JOURNEYS
OF THE
MIND

GW00506191

JOURNEYS
OF THE
MIND

Alan Pemberton

Paper Tiger

For John and Mark With Love

A Dragon's World Ltd Imprint

Dragon's World Ltd
Limpsfield
Surrey RH8 ODY
Great Britain

© Copyright Dragon's World Ltd 1983
© Copyright Illustrations for stories 1,5,7,11 and 12 Tom Adams 1983
© Copyright Illustrations for stories 2,3,4,6,8,9 and 10 Dragon's World Ltd 1983
© Copyright text Alan Pemberton 1983

No part of this book may be reproduced in any form or
by any electronic or mechanical means, including
information storage and retrieval systems, without
permission in writing from Dragon's World Limited,
except by a reviewer who may quote brief passages
in a review.

All rights reserved.

Caution. All images are copyright by Dragon's World Ltd
or by publishers acknowledged in the text. Their use
in any form without prior written permission from
Dragon's World Ltd, or the appropriate copyright
holder, is strictly forbidden.

Hardback: ISBN 0 905895 68 1
Limpback: ISBN 0 905895 67 3

Printed in Singapore

Contents

One

The Prospector

Illustrated by Tom Adams

Ben Lowry was a sixty-year-old prospector with no great love for his fellow man. He was a loner who experienced a greater fullness of spirit within nature's wilderness than he ever did in the company of people. He lived and worked at one with the harsh, demanding aridity of the Australian outback, neither admiring nor professing any love for that barren land which he combed for gold and precious stones. It was a working marriage between Ben, the husband and hunter, and nature, the elusive spouse. Ben liked his marriage. It demanded nothing of him emotionally and, physically, the life suited him. Slight and leathery, he almost blended with the landscape he inhabited and would certainly go un-noticed in a crowd. The only clue to the deep strength and tenacity of his character lay in his sharp brown eyes. They were not compassionate eyes – they were the eyes of a survivor.

He was a product of the great 1930s Depression, when men of all classes saw their jobs and lives collapse. They took to the roads, hills and mountains in search of work or any product of nature which could be sold or traded for life's necessities. These were the Australian swagmen and, when after those dark years sanity returned, many of them no longer desired to play the games of structured society. So they remained wanderers, treasuring independence above all else. Ruthless and cynical, Ben expected his fellow human beings to be dishonest – given half a chance – and experience had taught him they usually were.

With provisions enough for three months, Ben had driven three hundred miles into the bush north-east of Cannes, the small Queensland town where he had spent the previous night being thrown out of the bars. He had found a suitable camp site by the edge of a cool-flowing stream and was soon settled into his temporary home. The setting had a harsh, naked beauty. On either side of the river a thin line of silver-barked gum trees rustled gracefully in the breeze. These sturdy eucalyptus provided welcome shade during the intense heat of day, and in the evenings filled the air with a sweet aroma, a fragrance that once experienced is never forgotten. The stream itself, which hurried over colourful rocks and stones studding the smooth gravel of the river bed, was clear and unpolluted. Beyond, a carpet of mulga covered the dry earth. Short, brown and bushy, it stretched for as far as the eye could see. The flatness of the landscape was relieved now and then by huge red rocks which grew out of the earth like offspring of the mountain range slumbering on the horizon.

As evening fell around him, Ben fed both himself and his old dog Ned and, having prepared sleeping bag and tent for the night, he leaned against a tree-stump, pulled out his favourite pipe and reflected on his plans for the morrow. He would rise early and start panning at sun-up. Perhaps the stream which gurgled and flowed beside him might yield a small stone or two. For Ben trusted to luck – and throughout his life as a prospector it had given him the strength to rise each morning.

Although the air was still warm and humid, Ben lit a small fire, partly to discourage the mosquitoes and partly as a protection against the darkness which had gathered about him. The night was clear, and Ben soon knew he could expect the moon and stars for company.

Half an hour later, Ned's growling brought his attention to the strange ball of light which seemed to be rolling down the side of a distant hill. Ben watched, fascinated, as it pulsed and glowed then disappeared, leaving him staring at the spot where it had been. Shaking his head slowly, he turned his gaze once more into the flickering flames. Probably a gang of kangaroo hunters, he thought, poking idly at the fire. But Ned seemed to share little of his master's nonchalance. It was as if the dog sensed something, for the hairs on his back stood up and he bared his stained teeth menacingly.

Ben soon forgot the incident and after another pipeful of tobacco yawned, stretched and took a long look at the magnificent umbrella of stars which now sparkled above him. The thought of sleep flowed pleasantly into his mind. Ned, however, remained restless, now and then pricking up his ears and growling at something beyond the intense darkness. Ben cursed and snapped at the dog to be quiet, but he also strained his eyes and ears in the same direction. The animal's nervousness was catching. Yet, apart from the gurgling stream and the gentle rustle of the eucalyptus trees, he could hear nothing and it was too dark to see much. He cursed the mongrel again, hurling a stick at him for good measure. Ned cowed into the dust, but his eyes darted back and forth between his master and the outer darkness.

Ben climbed into his tent at about ten o'clock and was soon fast asleep. It must have been at least two hours later when Ned's frantic barking dragged him back into consciousness. Thick with sleep, groggy and annoyed, he dragged himself out of his sleeping bag and stuck his head through the tent flaps. His initial anger soon turned to fear when he saw a man silently approaching the tent camp. What the hell was anyone doing here – hundreds of miles from the nearest civilisation and at this time of night? Also, by no stretch of the imagination could his visitor be described as ordinary.

The stranger seemed to be surrounded by an aura of softly pulsating colours, reminding Ben of the ball of light he had seen earlier. He was abnormally large in stature, being at least seven feet tall and magnificently proportioned. One of the weirdest things about him was his clothing which resembled a thin silver skin that shimmered in the brilliant moonlight. As the visitor drew nearer the light about him seemed to fade.

Ben reached for his gun and poked the barrel through the tent flaps. "That's far enough. What do you want?"

The stranger stopped and answered very softly. "I come in peace. Do not be afraid."

The voice was oddly metallic. Prickling with fear, Ben jabbed the gun nervously at the stranger as he spoke. "That's far enough, mate. Who the hell are you?"

"I'm lost and I saw your fire. Do you mind if I rest for a while?" The stranger put his hand out to the dog and to Ben's surprise Ned stopped barking and began wagging his tail affably. Feeling a little easier now, Ben lowered the gun and climbed out of the tent.

"Lost, you say. Well, where's your transport?"

"Over there," said the stranger, pointing in the direction of the hills.

"That's funny. I saw a light over there earlier. Thought it was a bunch of roo hunters. Must have been you..." Ben's voice tailed away.

"What are you doing so far from your kind?" the man asked.

Ben thought the question odd, but, looking at the man's clothes again, concluded that he must be a foreigner. "I'm prospecting," he replied. "Gold, opals, rubies – that sort of thing. What about yourself?"

"I, too, am prospecting, but not for gold or precious stones."

Ben stared closely at the stranger before him. He appeared human in every sense but there was something wrong – something about his eyes. Ben began prodding at the fire with sharp nervous stabs.

"If you're not prospecting for gold, then what are you after?"

"Your race." replied the stranger quietly.

As Ben looked quizzically at him a piece of wood burst into flame, throwing a light over the man's face. It was then that Ben could see what was wrong with his eyes – they contained no pupils. For the first time in years the old prospector felt real terror.

"Look mate, I think you'd better move off back to where you came from – and quick!" Ben levelled his gun and cocked the hammer.

But the man with no pupils raised a hand. "I wish you no harm. But there are things we must know about your people. Therefore, I must ask you to come with me." He stood up and straightened to his full height. His huge frame was once more surrounded by coloured light.

"I'm going nowhere!" said Ben and, aiming the gun at the man's head, he fired off both barrels. To his utter amazement the stranger remained perfectly still, seemingly untouched by the blast.

The stranger stepped forward and took the gun from Ben's tremb-

ling hands. "If you will come with me, I will promise you a safe return. I will also give you more gold and jewels than you have ever seen."

To Ben's surprise, he turned to the dog and gently stroked him between the eyes. The animal crumpled without a sound. Terrified and bewildered, Ben tried to run, but the stranger was too quick for him.

"I wish you no harm," he repeated, touching the centre of Ben's forehead with a pulsing fingertip.

Ben groped his way out of a mental mist to hear Ned barking outside the tent. But where was his mysterious visitor? He chuckled when he realised that he had, after all, been dreaming. He crawled out of the tent and stretched luxuriously. Then he saw the gun and beside it the two spent cartridges. His spine ran cold. Glancing towards his old car, Ben noticed the amount of dust that had collected on the chassis. He looked back into the tent and saw that most of his food had rotted and that everything looked as if it had been deserted for weeks. Then, in a corner, Ben saw an unfamiliar box. He lifted the lid and saw that it was full of gold nuggets and precious stones. Standing trembling by the ruins of the camp, Ben tried to make sense of what had happened – and failed.

He wasted no time in breaking camp and heading for the nearest town. The incredible sequence of events was pushed to the back of his mind by sheer greed. Ben took a handful of the nuggets to the first dealer he came across and was paid handsomely, for it was metal of the finest quality. But when Ben had left the dealer's office, the clerk behind the desk turned to his colleague.

"Did you notice anything funny about that bloke?"

"Now that you mention it, there was something odd about him – about the way he looked at you. Something empty about his eyes."

"Yes," said the clerk. "They didn't have any pupils."

Eyes now closed, the man sat in the shady bar, the table beside him piled with empty glasses, while further down the dusty street two dogs squared up to each other. One was a great snarling brute with a dirty yellow coat and fangs to match, the other a small mongrel, grey-muzzled and wiry. The larger dog yelped in fear then ran, tail between his legs, his terrified howls reverberating through the still noon air.

Two

The Recluse

Illustrated by Graham Humphries

They couldn't have made a more unlikely couple; Tiang, the youngest daughter of a wealthy Malaysian trader and Paul, a highly-strung composer. At twenty she was placid and serene in that fatalistic manner of her race, whereas he, at thirty, a mixture of European, Russian and Jewish blood pounding through his veins, enjoyed nothing more than a running battle with the world and its inhabitants.

There was no question about it being love at first sight. Tiang had arrived to spend the weekend at my cottage, then situated near Hastings' beautiful fire hills. I had wished for some time to celebrate this wonderful area in verse and prose and Paul, who shared my passion for that unique terrain, was anxious to be involved musically. The idea of a documentary began to grow and Tiang, who was then studying new filming techniques in London, was highly recommended as "the girl with the different eye".

I regret to say that nothing of consequence arose from our collaboration except for some extraordinary upside-down, inside-out footage

which effectively disguised the natural glory of the fire hills and with it, my embryonic concept for a documentary. But soon after that weekend, Tiang gave up her studies in London, and to the horror of her family in Penang, went to live in Paul's lovely medieval house in Hastings.

Paul was both a natural and brilliant artist who at that time was fast becoming the most sought after young musician in the country. But it was a very different life for Tiang who suddenly found that she was living solely for Paul's work with little or no room left for her own. It was obvious to all who knew him that Paul was totally obsessed by Tiang's exquisite body, jet black shoulder length hair and classical Malaysian features. They seemed caught by fate in a creative if tumultuous relationship which gave them enormous involvement, passion and anguish and in which they were both apparently happy.

After a few months Tiang was summoned to the family home in Penang, ostensibly to take her holiday, but more importantly to explain to her parents just what she was up to. Naturally Paul ranted at her for deserting him when he needed her most but she calmly packed her cases and flew home, promising to return.

Tiang arrived on a morning flight and, exhausted, had been persuaded to spend most of the day resting. In the evening friends and family gathered to welcome her over a huge meal which the old cook had prepared with Tiang's favourite dishes in mind. It was a happy occasion and no mention of her mysterious life in England entered the conversation, although she knew that was certainly on her mother's agenda for a not too distant moment. Tiang had sat next to her father all evening. He had said little but beamed with satisfaction that his youngest and favourite daughter was again by his side. He was an old, comfortably fat, worldly man who had the habit of spending long periods in isolation, living in a small mountain shack above Penang. For as long as she could remember he had periodically retired from life, even during the height of his career as a merchant. It was something that all the family accepted for he gained strength and happiness from his isolation so his practice was to the benefit of everyone.

Tiang's homecoming had brought her father joyfully down from his mountain retreat. He loved her and could never see fault in anything she

19

did. He was totally untouched by her affair with Paul. Whilst his more conventional wife lamented their daughter's flagging morals, he was content to listen and smile. He made only one statement on the matter,

"She will love until she stops loving. If she does not stop loving then she has found happiness. What can be so wrong?"

His wife, although loving him deeply, would get irritated by his succinct logic. She preferred a more meaty emotional approach, coupled with a little seasoning of drama. Conclusions dissatisfied her unless they were her own.

So whilst Tiang's father enjoyed his daughter's lightness of spirit, her mother tried continually to extort promises from Tiang that she should put an end to her mad affair and return to family and studies.

One hot and sticky evening Tiang and her father sat alone on the verandah of the villa listening in silence to the exotic sounds of a tropical night. He was dressed, as usual, in a loose traditional robe, much frowned on by his wife, who preferred Western attire. Suddenly, the old man touched her arm.

"Tiang, I have met an old man in the hills. I know him well, his vision is deep and far, he sees things which others do not." He turned and smiled at her. "He has seen my death, child. I depart this world very soon,"

Tiang looked at him in horror, but the old man smiled again and took her hand.

"Come now, child, you're too young to worry over this nonsense about death," he said softly. "Do not feel sad. It is as natural as birth. Just as we come into this world as children, we enter another through death." He paused and laughed aloud. "And do you know, we are still children."

Tiang took his hand and held it tightly. She understood her father's words but her immense sorrow persisted. The old man felt her sadness and continued,

"It is our custom, as you know, to appear to one member of the family after death in order that they are assured our journey has been accomplished. I will come to you, Tiang. It will be you who knows first that I am in my new world."

"Father, I think it would be frightening to witness such a thing, yet I want it with all my heart."

"Do not fret, child, I will come to you in a manner unlikely to cause you fear."

Tiang asked her father if he would like her to remain in Malaysia so as to be near him, but the old man shook his head and smiled.

"You get on with your life and your love, my daughter. There is nothing you can do here but be unhappy waiting for my death."

So Tiang returned to England and resumed her life with the composer. Months passed and Tiang ceased to be preoccupied with the thought of her father's imminent death. Indeed, she began to wonder why he had bothered to discuss it with such conviction. After all, fortune tellers are sometimes wrong.

She had gone to bed one night leaving Paul deeply engrossed in his work. She read for a while and then slipped into a deep sleep. In the room below notes from the piano were interspersed with anguished silences as Paul struggled to find the elusive combination of mood and melody. Finally, at three thirty he staggered to bed. Paul's mind for a while remained so active that it could not be harnessed by sleep. He seemed to float through a miasma of contorted imagery. His disjointed thoughts were a confused mixture of fantasy and reality. Whether he fell asleep or not he could not tell, but suddenly the confused imagery gave way to a mental picture of great clarity. He saw a long road edged on either side by lush green trees and bushes which were more green and radiant than anything he had ever seen on Earth. There was music in the air – choral music more beautiful than anything he had ever heard. Then he saw a figure coming along the road towards him. He was fat and small and attired in a flowing garment with a vaguely oriental flavour. The figure stopped abruptly in the road, then waving his hand and smiling, turned around and walked into the distance. The picture faded and Paul knew nothing more until the morning light.

It was the memory of the music which made Paul recall the dream. It was so beautiful and so vivid in his mind that he told Tiang about it over breakfast. Her lovely face remained impassive whilst he raved about the ethereal quality of the sounds and colours. It had, he said, inspired him to write a symphony based on the colours of other worlds. Tiang stiffened

and suddenly became distant and sad.

"Was the man small and fat?" she asked softly.

"Yes, and he seemed very pleased with himself."

"How was he dressed?"

"In a loose sort of gown. Oriental-looking. Why do you ask?"

"I think, my love, you may have glimpsed another world last night." Then she closed her eyes and said quietly, "Thank you, my father, I am not fearful."

Three

The Bus

Illustrated by Bill Donohue

The old bus rolled and bounced along the rough track rattling its passengers like coins in a collection box. The drought had persisted and the landscape for as far as the eye could see was parched and barren. Stark dead trees, bleached by the relentless sun, stood white against the blue African sky, like gnarled alien hands from the realms of science fiction.

Inside the bus the stifling heat and discomfort had lulled the occupants into a resigned lethargy. Even the children lay quiet in the arms of their exhausted parents. There was nothing to be done but suffer another hundred miles to reach a destination few would envy. For they were migrant workers, on the move with family and possessions to a new mine in the Transvaal and promise of work and a place to stay.

Sitting trace-like in the back was an old woman. Brown and leathery, she was well into her eighties and the mother of one of the workers. Barely uttering a word, she was content to gaze out of the window, seeming to find peace, even beauty, in the arid landscape. For with the tranquil dignity of old age came the certain knowledge that this would be her final journey.

As evening approached the bus halted at a small village where a few trees and the trickling remnants of a once broad river offered a refreshing welcome to the exhausted travellers. The inhabitants looked on impassive as children and adults gasped and squealed with pleasure revelling in its delicious coolness. The villagers' cautious hospitality could extend to no more than the basic gifts of shade and water, for their life too had become intolerably hard.

The old woman sat in the shade of a tree, her serenity undisturbed by the excitement around her. As the blistering sun cooled to a glowing cherry-coloured disc, she became restless, sniffing the air like a dog and turning this way and that as if looking for something.

"What is it mother?" asked her son. "Is there anything you need?"

She ignored him and, turning to one of the villagers, said, "There is evil here. There is a sick one in your midst."

"No, old woman. There is no sickness here," replied the man. "You feel the pains of a woman in labour. Her time is near, that is all."

"So is her death!" said the old woman, unshakable authority in her voice. "Take me to her."

"Do you know something about childbirth, old woman?"

"I know something about evil!" she said flatly.

He led her across the village and into a small dome-shaped hut. On a pile of rush mats a young woman groaned and writhed as a series of violent contractions racked her body.

"A day and a night. The child will not come. Still she moans but it will not come."

"Would you hurry it into death?"

"What are you saying, old woman? The child is not yet born, why speak of death?"

"Inside the mother the child lives, but in the world it will die. Where is the medicine man? I would speak to him."

The man shrugged his shoulders resignedly and together they left the hut. As they walked across the village compound the still evening was pierced by a high-pitched wailing cry. The old woman stopped and looked in the direction from which the eerie sound was coming. Swaying beneath a tree like a cobra about to strike was a young man. The almost inhuman keening pouring from him was accompanied by the rhythmic thud of his war club striking the ground.

"Who is that?" she asked.

"That is Bala, the woman's husband. He shares the pains of his wife."

"Not for long," said the old woman. "Where is the medicine man?"

Her guide led her to a small bony figure seated cross legged before a circle of skulls. His eyes were closed as if in a trance. She regarded him for a moment then hurled a strange word into his stillness. The man's head snapped up and he stared at her intently.

"Why do you stop the spirit on its journey?"

"The Great Ones of the sky want it so," he replied. "I have spoken."

"And do the Great Ones tell you to take the soul of the child?"

"I have spoken," repeated the medicine man, closing his eyes as if to resume his meditation.

"Do they ask also for the soul of the mother? She is dying with her pains. What harm has she done?"

"The Great Ones have so commanded, old woman. Beware that you do not stand between them and their purpose."

She looked carefully at the placing of the skulls, then spoke again.

"I do not believe the Great Ones want a soul. I believe that you, old man, seek revenge." She regarded him fiercely. "The skulls speak of evil, who do you avenge with the death of this child?"

"Go, old woman, before it is too late for you."

"You cannot frighten me," she said with scorn. "I too am of the knowledge."

The medicine man dismissed this with a wave of his hand. "You? How can you be of the knowledge? You are a woman. Women are not of the knowledge!"

"Your vanity, old man, is the cause of the evil here. It is not the Great Ones who have spoken, it is your pride."

He flew into a violent rage, shaking his fist at the terrified villager who had brought the woman to him. "Fool, take the old hag away," he

shrieked. "She's crazy, take her away!"

"I'll go when I'm finished," said the old woman with great dignity. "Let the small soul end its journey. You punish the unborn because you are jealous of the marriage. You wanted her, old man, wanted her for yourself. Pride, power and vanity have blinded you to the truth, which is that you are old and spent, just as I am. Ask yourself, what life could a young woman have with you?"

The medicine man became deadly silent. Then he picked up a bone and caressed it menacingly, his lips curled with dreadful hatred. She knew what was coming.

"Beware you do not go too far, lest you never speak again."

"I have lived too long to be frightened by a vain old man. I command you to break the spell and let the young soul through."

"You?" snarled the medicine man. "You command me?"

"If you value your life you will do as I ask."

He pointed the bone at the woman's head and, piercing her with his dark eyes, muttered a stream of strange malevolent words. The villager who had been standing nearby covered his eyes and ran away howling like a wolf; the bone meant certain death.

But there was no trace of fear upon the old woman's face. She bent down slowly, picked up one of the seven skulls and walked back to the hut where the young girl still writhed in agony. Placing it on the ground between the girl's legs, the old woman cupped her head in her hands and appeared to go into a trance. For a time she was silent and, despite the lingering heat and humidity outside, the hut became icy cold, so much so that the woman who was assisting the birth shivered uncontrollably. The old woman's hands began to travel over the pregnant girl's body. She did not physically touch her but made long sweeping gestures just above the skin, uttering as she did so a stream of soft cabbalistic words. After a while a great peace fell about the pregnant girl. The old woman rose and cried aloud to the heavens.

"Great Ones, as one enters, so two shall leave."

The girl screamed and gasped as the baby began to grope its way onto the plains of Earth. It was all over very quickly, the village woman assisting the birth tying off the umbilical cord then severing it with a

knife. As the child took his first breaths of air, the old woman collapsed dead to the floor.

A strange heavy darkness fell about the village and distant thunder grumbled in the heavens. People stared apprehensively towards the sky and one by one crept silently into their huts. Suddenly, the husband, who was now sitting moaning beneath the tree, rose to his feet. His face was expressionless as he raised the war club above his head. Then, letting out a blood-curdling roar, he hurtled towards the old medicine man. There could be no question that the man was possessed as he delivered seven brutal but precise blows, shattering the old man's skull.

In the silent hut mother and child shared an exhausted peace. Beside them lay the old woman, looking more asleep than dead. The woman who had assisted the birth was staring intently – not at the corpse or the mother and child, but at the skull which the old woman had placed between the mother's legs. She had heard an agonising howl from outside the hut, then watched in astonishment as it had shattered under what appeared to be the force of seven invisible blows. Two souls for two the old woman had bargained and in her death lay her victory.

Later, as the bus lurched and rolled on its journey, something happened, something which turned tragedy into soft joy. A gentle rain fell upon the baked Transvaal for the first time in months and the parched earth surrendered to it with a grateful sigh.

Four

The Millionaire

Illustrated by Graham Humphries

It was the most tragic industrial accident in the uneventful history of Sweden. The explosion at the armaments factory came as no surprise to the people who worked there. They had complained for months about the critical need for new safety measures in respect of the dangerous new weapons they were producing, but the management, working under strict orders to cut back on capital expenditure, fobbed them off by saying that a proper research programme was to be conducted to establish the precise nature of the new safety requirements. The results of this stalling were fifty men blown to bits and hundreds more maimed for life.

The man responsible for the fatal cutbacks had been the chairman and major shareholder, Dr Alfred Richter, a twice-over millionaire who had the Swedish establishment securely in the palm of his hand. Richter had felt no real grief for those who had been injured or killed. War and death were, after all, his business, however indirectly. As for a conscience, he had never developed, or even felt the need for one. As a child he had received instructions, not love. He had been privately tutored and segregated from the normal world until early manhood. With a brain exclusively conditioned to fact and logic, he suffered none of the anxieties or elations which arise from the seesaw of human emotion for, having been born into a family with sufficient money and influence, he had never wanted for anything. As a result, Dr Richter was incapable of emotion; he simply didn't know what it meant.

Richter was an odd-looking man in late middle age, with a slight, almost feminine build. His small face was pinched and nondescript – an empty canvas awaiting the brush strokes of inspiration; totally expressionless, a brilliant walking computer clothed in human flesh.

At university, Richter had won honours in chemistry and engineering. Later, he joined the family armaments empire and within five years had taken over from his father, having proved himself to be a faultless administrator and ruthless despot. He was neither cruel nor kind, and this cold neuter quality had a strangely terrifying effect on those who knew him socially or worked under him.

Part of Richter's family duties entailed producing a son and heir who, like himself, would eventually be expected to devote his life to the business. He married three times. There was no issue from the first brief marriage, to a young English heiress. She divorced him after a year of excruciating boredom. His second wife was a beautiful Swedish actress. Her life changed from fun in the glittering world of theatre to misery in the rigours of social etiquette. By insisting that she conformed to a life of suffocating ritual, he destroyed her spirit. She became a hopeless alcoholic and finally took her shattered life by cutting her wrists in a bath. Again there was no issue.

Wife number three was different. Helen Rakanstic was like Richter, for money and power mattered more to her than anything else. Herself the product of a rich American oil family, Helen saw profit in the marriage and couldn't give a damn about his extraordinary lack of sensitivity. She was quite happy flitting around the world at Richter's expense and maintaining a variety of houses in the world's sunspots. There was a mutual understanding, for Helen was the only woman who had realised that Dr Richter harboured a revulsion for the opposite sex and avoided any physical contact. She discovered very quickly that he was totally asexual, and as she despised him she merely took lovers to compensate herself. Needless to say, there was no issue.

After the accident in the factory, life changed dramatically for both of them. The threats on their lives became so frequent that they were forced to leave Sweden and take up residence in England. The Richters lived on a vast secluded estate in Northamptonshire with an army of maids, cooks, butlers and gardeners. Still a major shareholder, he continued to run the family empire in Sweden, then Helen began to suffer from agoraphobia.

At first it was simply a terror of leaving the house, but Helen's world diminished as her fears increased and in a very short time she became incapable of leaving her bedroom. This mental condition carried with it another that had developed with terrifying intensity – total hatred of Dr Alfred Richter.

She wanted revenge for her lost years of womanhood, since she had always felt stronger and more capable than any man she had ever met. To her men were boys, grown boys, who women had allowed, nay encouraged, to believe were cleverer and stronger than they. It was to her an illusion; she knew which of the sexes held the true strength and she was sick of living the lie that suggested otherwise. She intended to make "unfeeling" Richter "feel" even if it was only misery and pain.

His daily visits to her room began as a courtesy which quickly grew into a sinister ritual. She had their handyman fix an intercom connecting his study with her bedroom. At precisely 4pm each day she would buzz Richter and summon him to her presence. He soon knew what to expect and in a strange inexplicable way he began to enjoy it. He would respond to the summons like a man conditioned by hypnosis to react to a certain sound or gesture. The intercom would buzz and he would immediately leave his study and ascend the huge curving staircase to her room. He would say nothing on entering – for he had no reason to. Always seated in the same chair, her legs covered by a blanket, she would start the day's theme of hate.

One day, a year after the accident, she was particularly vicious.

"You disgust me. Do you know that? You utterly disgust me. Look at your pathetic body. How can you ever be seen as a man. You can't even perform the natural acts of a man. You're like a corpse – like one of the people who died in your explosion." Helen curled her lips cruelly and her blue eyes burned with hate. "Tell me, Doctor, do you ever think about the people you killed? Does it mean anything – anything at all to you?"

"How could it? It was an accident," he replied slowly. "Anyway, what is death? It comes to us all eventually."

"I want to see death when it comes to you. I want to watch you die slowly. I want to relish every minute of your final agony. Then I want to see the life drain out of you and smell the air of a world without you in it."

But this time Richter gave as good as he got.

"I married you for children, and you failed me. You have no purpose left in my life except that I find your new-found madness slightly more amusing than your years of sanity."

"Children!" She rocked back and forth with angry mocking laughter. "Children! I aborted three of your children!"

For the first time since they met his face betrayed a flicker of emotion and she clapped her hands with triumph.

"What did you say?" he muttered, quickly clearing his face of expression.

"I said I aborted three of your children. As soon as I knew I was pregnant I terminated them."

He stared at her blankly. "Why would you do such a thing? What was the logic?"

"Logic! Did you think I ever wanted anything of yours growing in my body."

Despite his anger Richter was pedantic. "You had no right! The Richter empire needs an heir. It was part of our marriage agreement that you had children. Now you tell me this shameful news."

She threw back her head and laughed again. "Shameful news," she mimicked. "Balls. You didn't think it shameful when over fifty men died in an explosion that you were too damn mean to prevent. You deal in death, Richter – another three won't trouble you."

"I want a divorce." But Richter sounded as if he was addressing a board meeting.

"Well, you ain't getting it! Anyway, honey, let's face it, you couldn't afford the publicity. Now, get out!"

Richter clenched his fists and stamped his foot like a child. He was utterly lost for words and looked so ridiculously out of character that Helen sobbed with hysterical laughter until he turned and stamped out of the room. As he slammed the door he heard her voice shrill from the other side of the heavy wood:

"Don't forget, sugar, same time tomorrow."

For months she kept up this relentless assault on his character, each time forcing him ever deeper into realms of sensation he had never experienced. He felt hatred for her but it was tempered with a compelling fascination. After each ordeal he would go back to his study and relive every hateful word. He could never understand why it was that they made him glow with an emotion bordering on pleasure. By attempting to destroy the Dr Richter she so reviled, she was creating somebody else. For the first time in his life he was involved in a real relationship.

Richter found his mind could no longer concentrate on matters regarding business but was obsessed with the agoraphobic who lived in the bedroom upstairs. He would sit in his study, a room equipped with every conceivable aid for international communication and dream up the most hideous methods of destroying her. Like a little boy relishing an imaginary triumph over the school bully, he would snigger and rub his hands together if a particularly clever plot occurred to his warped and devious mind.

Sometimes she was asleep or "too busy" to perform her ritual flaying of his psyche. Then his immediate elation at having escaped the torture would change to another new emotion, something akin to disappointment. The uncertainty made the suspense of waiting for her summons all the sweeter.

After a while there were fears that Richter's judgement was failing, for where he had always been ruthlessly efficient he was becoming downright unreliable, being totally absorbed in his new world of exquisitely novel sensations. The lid was off and the result was a thoroughly confused man who didn't realise that he was becoming a slave to masochism.

One hot July afternoon as he sat working at his desk he sensed that he was not alone. He was gripped by sudden apprehension. Someone was standing in front of him and he had no desire to know who it was.

"Good afternoon, Dr Richter."

The chilling voice was deep and sonorous. The millionaire froze at the very sound of it, and continued to stare at his desktop.

"I don't know who you are and I have no wish to find out. Go away."

"Come, come, Doctor, that's not a very polite way to treat someone who has travelled far to give you a message."

Full of dreadful foreboding, Richter slowly raised his head and stared with utter amazement at the man who stood smiling before him. There could be no doubt that he was an undertaker, for he was dressed entirely in black and wore a tall Dickensian top hat. His face was skeletal and as he removed his gloves Richter winced with revulsion for his hands were mere bones with a thin covering of yellow skin.

"How did you get into my house?" he asked, rising unsteadily to his feet. "Nobody comes to my house without an appointment."

"I do not need an appointment with you, Dr Richter, for you already have one with me."

"Who are you?"

The undertaker smiled hideously. "A messenger."

"From whom?"

"Isn't it obvious to a man of your intellect?"

"Your ludicrous costume reminds me of an undertaker."

"Merely a symbol of my work. I've long ceased to be concerned with burial. My work is simply to deliver the message."

He raised his top hat and bowed gracefully, exposing as he did so a skull covered by the same revolting film of yellow skin. Richter's terror became rage and he slammed his fist upon the desk.

"Damn you, man," the shout emerged as a strangled squeak. "What message?"

"Oh, yes, the message." The vile-looking man smiled, glanced heavenward and put the top hat reverently to his chest.

"Dr Alfred Richter, I am here to inform you that your name has been called and that on the nineteenth day, one months hence, you will have an

appointment with death. It will be the last appointment you will ever need to honour.''

"Another threat!'' Richter screamed hysterically. "Another damn threat from the victims of that explosion.'' He calmed himself and leered knowingly at the man in black. "So that's why they sent you, dressed in those vulgar clothes and looking like death. You're one of them! You're part of the vile campaign of terror,'' He grabbed a small bell and rang it furiously. "Threaten me in my own house would you? Well, you'll never leave here except under police guard.''

"You are wasting your time, Doctor. I am nothing to do with the people you burned and maimed. I am merely here to inform you of the inevitable fact of your death and final judgement. Remember, one month hence. Prepare well, you have much to answer for.''

Richter turned his head as the butler entered the room. "Call the police, I want this fiend arrested.''

The butler gazed at the millionaire in astonishment. "Fiend, sir?''

"Him, blockhead,'' he screamed, pointing but not looking to the spot where the man in black stood.

"With respect, Sir, there doesn't appear to be a fiend in the room.''

Richter turned and looked at the empty space before him. "But he was there, standing right there.''

"Well, he appears to have left, Sir.''

"How could he have left, fool? There's only one door and he was here when you walked through it.'' He slumped into his chair. "I suppose you'll tell me you didn't let him into my study unannounced.''

"There have been no visitors at all today, Sir.''

Richter turned and snarled at the immaculate bastion of discretion who stood straight-backed by the door. "It's her, isn't it? You're conspiring with her.'' His voice again became squeaky as paranoia fuelled hysteria. "You think you can drive me insane and take over my empire? You fools, I'll...''

He was frozen in mid-sentence by the buzz of the intercom. Mesmerised, he pressed the button. It was Helen.

"It's four o'clock, Jerk. Get up here,'' she purred with menacing warmth. "I've got a few things I want to discuss with you!''

He left the room like a zombie and climbed the stairs to experience yet again the mental flagellation which had now become the highlight of his day. This session, however, would be different, for he imagined he had something rather special with which to parry her insane acrimony.

She was slumped rather than seated in her usual chair. An empty sherry decanter, a half-filled glass and a slurred voice suggested that she'd had more than enough to drink.

"So, what's new, Jerk? You look a touch flaky. Don't tell me somebody's upset that sensitive little soul of yours?"

"You are a fool if you think you can drive me insane with your infantile games."

"You mean you won't play Russian Roulette for me today. Pity, I was wondering what your brains would look like spread all over the carpet. I wonder how many people had their brains blown out in your little explosion."

"Your constant references to that stupid accident are as boring as that man you arranged for me to see today. I am not frightened by your futile threat of death."

"Why would I bother to threaten you, Jerk? Don't you know that you're more use to me alive. What would I do without my little playmate coming to see me every day?"

"So you deny sending that ridiculous undertaker to see me?"

She looked at him incredulously for a moment then rocked backwards and forwards convulsing in raucous laughter. "Undertaker? What in hell are you talking about?"

"You know damn well. The man you sent to inform me that I would be dead one month from today. I must congratulate you on your choice of actors. With the collaboration of the butler he did a most impressive disappearing act. Naturally I'm taking steps to sack the butler and – "

Helen laughed louder and louder. At the pathetic man who stood before her looking so serious and at the nonsense he was speaking.

"You're flipping, Jerk, do you know that? You're flipping!"

Richter flushed with rage and clenched his fists. "You're lying! You disgusting bitch. You sent him. I wish you would die. I hate you. I hate you." Then his hands made a throttling gesture. "One day I'll..."

She stopped laughing and addressed him with deep contempt. "One day you'll what, freak? Kill me? You wouldn't have the manhood to."

He calmed himself and straightened his jacket. "I hope that you're satisfied now that you have disturbed my afternoon's work with your childish games. If you'll excuse me I shall return to my study."

She smiled, lit a cigarette and blew a cloud of smoke in his direction, knowing that the smell would nauseate him. He furiously waved away the smoke and turned to leave the room.

"Tell me, freak. Isn't there a character in Swedish folklore that's supposed to visit people and warn them just before they die?"

"You should know. After all you sent him to me today."

"What do they call him?"

"The undertaker."

"Well, well!"

"Do you still refuse to admit that it was a stupid plan of yours intended to unnerve me?"

She batted her eyelashes, smiled and, in the accent of a Southern Belle, drawled, "Now why would I want you dead or even frightened, Honey-pie? Just think of all the fun I'd be missing if you weren't here."

"American slut!"

"Give my love to the undertaker."

As the days of the following month passed, Dr Richter became more and more uneasy. He had the nineteenth of August ringed in red on his calendar – for this day was apparently to be his last. There was to be no sleep for him on the night of the eighteenth. Instead, Richter suffered hours of terror, filled with nightmares of the dead and injured caused by the explosion.

Then came the blessed light of day, and as he took his usual cup of coffee in the study he smiled smugly to himself. After all, this was supposed to be the day of his death, yet here he was fit and well, drinking his coffee.

Richter passed the morning euphorically working at his desk and even ordered his favourite Swedish steak dish to be prepared and a bottle of vintage claret to be brought from the cellar. He would lunch well and drink to his next twenty years. Just before entering the dining room he

had an impish thought. Giggling in anticipation, he pressed the intercom button.

"Yeah?"

"Good afternoon, my American slut."

"What do you want, Jerk?"

"I thought you might be pleased to find me still alive, my sweet spitting viper."

"You'll wish you were dead when I've finished with you today. See you at four, freak."

He giggled again as he padded off to the oak-panelled dining room where, at one end of a long gleaming table, a solitary place had been perfectly laid.

It was unlike him to have fallen asleep after lunch but the good food and wine, combined with the heat of the day and his favourite armchair had lulled Richter into a comfortable oblivion. Then he heard, as if from a distance, his study clock softly chime three o'clock. Opening his eyes, he sat for a while collecting his thoughts. Thinking that tea would be refreshing he rose to ring for the butler but as he picked up the bell he became aware of the sound of horses' hooves. This was not uncommon in the country but there was something different about these horses for they were crunching on gravel and there was no gravel on his drive or the road at the bottom of it.

The sound grew louder and louder until curiosity forced him to the window. Terror, shock, fear and disbelief merged in his mind and froze him to the spot. For through the window he saw, approaching the house, a wonderfully ornate hearse pulled by magnificent, black-plumed horses, silver headdresses gleaming in the sun.

As the hearse crunched to a halt outside the entrance to the house, the driver looked straight at the millionaire gazing at him in horror through his study window. The same black suit and top hat. There could be no doubt who it was. Richter turned away as the grotesque figure beckoned him with his deathly, skeletal hand.

"No, no, it can't be," he screamed, covering his face with his hands. Then he heard the sound of a whip crack and more crunching of gravel.

He looked again to see the hearse thundering down his drive towards the main road.

Rushing out of the room he yelled for the butler who raced to him.

"Did you see it this time?" he raved.

"See what, Sir?"

"Don't lie to me. I shouldn't have allowed you to work out your notice. You're in league with my wife..."

"Sir, I don't understand."

"Liar! Out of my way."

Richter raced down the drive in a frenzy of anger and terror, plunging out of the gates and into the road.

He had no chance. The driver thrashed the horses on as the hearse hurtled and thundered towards him. Before he could be trampled to death one of them had lowered its head, impaling Richter's skull on the spiked silver mount worn as part of its ornate headdress.

A few moments later a confused butler raced to the scene of the accident. He had heard a terrible screech of tyres and a dreadful sickening thud. The chauffeur of the Rolls Royce was bending over the body. He looked up, pale and shaking. His hands sketched a gesture of despair.

"He just ran straight out into the road. I didn't have a chance to... God, look at his face."

The butler did and saw the jagged hole between the eyes. "I had to pull him off the car."

The chauffeur shuddered at the memory. "But how could that ever pierce a skull?" he asked, pointing at the figure of "Ecstasy" on the Rolls Royce's bonnet.

At four o'clock precisely the intercom in Dr Alfred Richter's study buzzed like an angry wasp, then Helen's impatient voice ripped through the speaker. "Come on up, Jerk, it's playtime. Wait till you hear what I've got to say to you. You'll just die..."

Five

Chance Meeting

Illustrated by Tom Adams

There was a spring in Paul Langham's step as he walked briskly along Eastbourne promenade towards the pier. The day was sparkling fresh and the bright autumn sunlight danced on the smooth surface of the ocean. A pleasant amalgam of sea smells pervaded the air as people strolled and talked amicably to each other. Having no great appetite for lunch he decided to visit his favourite place at the end of the pier. It was nothing fancy, just a pleasant little bar with an uninterrupted view of the sea. It was a reminder of childhood holidays, a place to reflect.

When he entered the bar he was surprised to find it much busier than usual. He bought himself a beer and seeing no empty tables sat down opposite an attractive woman in her early thirties.

She began to fidget uneasily in her chair and seemed intensely conscious of his presence. After a few moments of uneasy silence he felt compelled to say something – anything – to break the tension.

"You don't mind if I sit here?" It sounded lame.

"Not in the least," she replied.

"Sorry, I had the feeling I was making you feel uncomfortable. It's not normally as full as this," he said, looking around as nonchalantly as possible. "Usually there are plenty of tables."

When his gaze returned to the woman he found her staring directly at him, longing in her eyes. Now it was his turn to feel uncomfortable. What was it about her?

"Should I know you?" he asked.

She smiled softly.

"Well, it's not that you look familiar," he continued awkwardly, "it's just that I feel as if I should. Are you local?"

"No," she said picking up her glass, "I'm from the North."

"So am I," he said. "Manchester. I was born in Manchester."

"I know."

"How could you?" he asked with genuine surprise.

"Your accent."

"Oh yes, of course, I sometimes forget that I've still got one." He paused and then asked, "So, where are you from?"

"Manchester," she replied.

"There you are then. Perhaps that's where I've met you before."

"Perhaps," There was a touch of sadness in her voice.

"Are you on holiday?"

"No, I'm here to see someone – someone very dear."

For a while conversation stopped as both of them gazed out to sea, the initial feeling of awkwardness evaporated.

Then it was her turn to ask the questions. She suddenly wanted to know everything about him and Paul was more than happy to oblige her.

He told her he had been orphaned as a boy after a road accident had killed his parents. Reared by his grandparents, he had worked hard and won a scholarship to Leicester University. With a degree in law he eventually moved South to take up a partnership in a firm of solicitors.

He chatted on happily for there was something about her which encouraged him to talk about personal matters which he wouldn't normally have discussed with a stranger. But she didn't feel like a stranger.

All the time he spoke, the woman was silent. He stopped talking abruptly and felt rather embarrassed at the amount he had told her in so short a time. She seemed to understand.

"Did you marry?"

"Yes. A girl I met at university."

"And children?"

"Three girls. I have photographs. Would you like to—"

"Oh, please. Yes I would."

He took a photograph out of his wallet. Her hand shook slightly as she took it from him. He pointed in turn to the three pretty girls.

"Amanda, Karen and Nicky."

"Oh, but they're beautiful – so beautiful! How old are they?"

"Twelve, ten and nine."

As she handed the photo back to him he noticed that she was avoiding his eyes. Then she reached into her bag, pulled out a tissue and blew her nose gently. He could see that she was trying to hold back tears.

"Are you okay? Has something upset you?"

"Sometimes people cry with joy" she said, still avoiding his eyes.

She put the tissue back in her bag then leaned over and touched his hand. His whole body tingled. Not a sexual reaction, but something he had never felt until now. Here was a woman who he had never seen before creating in him the most turbulent emotions.

Then she stood up and looked at him for a moment, and for the first time he was able to see her fully. She appeared handsome rather than beautiful, and her face radiated serenity. Her black eyes and neat dark hair were perfect and nothing about her seemed out of proportion. Her clothes did seem a little odd, though. Nothing obvious, just somehow off-key. She picked up her handbag.

"Have you some time?" she asked.

"Well yes, but not much. I have a client at three. Why do you ask?"

"I want you to come with me. There's something I must show you. It won't take long."

Although confused by her request he did not for one second question her. As they left the bar, Langham had the uneasy feeling that this had been no chance meeting. If only he could remember where on earth he had seen her before. Knowing neither where they were going nor why,

Langham was sure of only one thing – that he had never in his life felt more comfortable with any living person than he did now with the woman walking beside him.

"Isn't it strange..." she said, suddenly stopping and peering down through the spaces between the wooden planks of the pier.

"I don't understand," he said, looking in the same direction.

"Strange how childhood memories suddenly come alive again. I used to get such weird feelings seeing the water through those cracks. So far away to a child. Just like walking on water."

"Ah yes," he said breaking into a grin. "I remember that. I was always absolutely sure that at any moment they'd have to give way and down, down, down I'd go."

"I remember," she said quietly as they walked on.

A warm smell, thick and sticky-sweet, wafted over them.

"Candy floss," she said excitedly, "You love candy floss. Come on, I'll buy you some."

"Candy floss," he laughed. "I haven't had candy floss in years."

"Well all the more reason why you should have it now then."

He simply couldn't believe his eyes as the man behind the counter whirled the sticks and conjured up two bulbous cotton creations.

She paid him and stuck one firmly in Langham's hand.

"Eat and enjoy," she said with a wicked smile.

They were sauntering rather than walking now. Then she insisted that they entered amusement arcades and play the most ridiculous of slot machines. His embarrassment dissolved after a while as he was caught up in her sense of fun. He hadn't really let himself go in years, but now he was a boy again and loving every minute of it. He did, however, draw the line at riding a monstrous "Mother Goose" but practically collapsed with laughter when she hitched up her skirts, climbed onto the great white bird and rode it with panache.

By the time they had passed through the exit turnstile and began walking along the sunny promenade, Paul Langham felt more relaxed and happy then ever before. Although he didn't want to break the spell, he was still confused by his emotions towards her.

"I have to tell you," he said uncomfortably. "Well, it's only fair to tell you, that I am a happily married man. I mean, I don't normally – "

"I know!" she said putting a finger on his lips, "I expect nothing of you. Just be happy for an hour."

"I don't understand. I really don't understand you – but for what it's worth, I feel happier than I can remember."

"You will understand soon," she said softly, "I promise you, you will understand soon! Now, I want you to take me for a trip in that rowing boat."

"But I haven't been rowing for years!"

"Didn't you say your greatest ambition was to go to sea?"

"No, I didn't say any such thing," he said looking at her curiously, "But how did you know that was always what I dreamed as a boy?"

"Call it woman's intuition," she said, suddenly grabbing his arm and pulling him down the steps towards the group of boats on the beach.

The water was clear and smooth and after a few clumsy mistakes, Langham fell into a pleasant rhythm which propelled the little boat gently through it. After a while, during which they had remained silent, he looked at his watch.

"Good God, the time. It's half past two. I've got a client at three."

"No you haven't."

"Look, it's been great fun, but business is business. I really must be getting back!"

"I'm your client!"

"What?"

"Somebody requiring advice on a trust?"

"Well, yes but why all…"

"You'll understand. I did say there was something I wanted you to see. Let's go then."

Once back on the promenade he began to feel edgy and confused.

"It would be helpful if you could explain what all this is about," he said, for the first time affecting a professional air.

"I can't tell you now," she said, taking his arm affectionately. "We need a taxi, darling. You'll understand soon."

"Darling." Why was she calling him "darling", but more important-ly why did it sound so natural and comforting? They strolled along the pavement until he spotted and hailed a passing cab. She gave the driver an address and for the short journey they sat in silence. Their destination turned out to be a large Victorian terraced house – one of many in a wide street which Langham did not recognise.

He paid the fare and turning to his companion he smiled. "I've just realised, I don't even know your name."

"It's not important. Come on."

They climbed the steps and entered the cool building. Inside a man was painting the hall. He nodded and seemed to look quizzically at them as they passed.

"This way," she said, leading him up the stairs.

When they reached the first floor they walked along a passage until they reached a door marked seven. She turned the doorknob and as the door opened she gestured for him to go in. He thought it odd that she had left it unlocked but then everything about that afternoon had been a little strange.

His stomach knotted into a tight ball of panic at what he saw. Then he heard a voice from behind him utter the words he would never forget. "Don't be frightened! Remember, I love you Paul..." He looked back but there was no one there, then turned again to stand rooted to the threshold, slack-jawed with disbelief.

It was as if he had been transported back in time thirty years. The room at which he gazed in astonishment was the very sitting room in which he had grown up as a boy in his parents' house. Everything – the carpets, curtains, furniture and ornaments – screamed memories of the happy childhood spent in Manchester before he was orphaned by that dreadful accident. On the mantelpiece stood a picture of himself and beside it one of his mother and father. He grabbed the photo of his parents and studied it closely. There could be no doubt now as to who the mysterious woman was. But his Mother was dead, damn it! He'd been to her funeral. He turned again and looked for the woman but there was no one there. He ran like a madman down the stairs and out of the building. But she was not to be seen.

Mind reeling, and gasping for breath, he returned to the house, and caught sight of the man they had passed earlier painting the wall.

"Did you see a woman leave?"

"Woman," said the man, "what woman?"

"The woman I came here with. You must have seen us."

"I saw you but I didn't see no woman," he said, looking Langham up and down suspiciously.

"Don't be ridiculous. Of course you must have seen her. She was wearing a blue hat and dress; a full dress with lots of petticoats…"

He stopped suddenly and thought about the dress and the style of the woman's coat and hat. Now he realised what had been so strange about her clothes. They bore no resemblance to current fashion, but belonged to another time – the time in which his Mother had died.

"Is something wrong?" asked the man. "You look a bit bothered."

"Do you mind if I take a look at number seven?"

"Why didn't you say," said the man, climbing down the ladder. "I couldn't work out why you just passed me like that. You're the one that wants to view the flat."

He led the way upstairs and along to number seven. Taking a huge bundle of keys out of his pocket he unlocked the door.

"Might smell a bit musty like, but it's been empty for a couple of weeks. Wife was going to polish the floor but her back went…" The man's voice faded into nothingness as the incredulous eyes of Paul Langham gazed into a totally empty room….

Six

The Barn

Illustrated by Bill Donohue

Robert Shaw was driving along a stretch of bleak road that ran across Cornwall's Bodmin Moor. A businessman, he was returning to London after a meeting. His deal had gone especially well and a substantial contract for his firm's computer hardware sat snug and signed in his pigskin briefcase.

Too much food and too much brandy had given him indigestion and his eyes were heavy as they scanned the road ahead of him. Even with little traffic it would be hours before he'd reach London. Perhaps it might be better if he stopped off at a hotel for the night and continued tomorrow. But the decision was unnecessary, however, for the engine cut out without even a warning splutter and his car glided to a halt by the side of the road.

"Damn and blast it!" He turned the ignition key aggressively. The engine was dead.

He stared out of the car and was amazed by the absolute blackness

surrounding him. To a city man the intense inkwell of a country night was almost beyond comprehension.

He was feeling anything but comfortable and although at first not actually afraid, he was rather more than concerned about his immediate position. He considered the options open to him. He could either sleep in the back seat until morning, though he didn't relish the prospect, or find a telephone and call for help.

Having been schooled in positive thinking, Shaw pulled a flashlight from the glove compartment and stepped outside. The wind tore into him like an icy razor, and he wrapped his overcoat more snugly round him. To add to his problems it was mid-December and snow had been forecast. The fear of being stranded in the snow quickened his step as he headed towards a light which he had noticed some distance away along the deserted road.

He kept hoping, almost praying now, that he would see the comforting beams of a car. He strained his ears above the howling wind for the reassuring sounds of a fellow traveller who might give him a lift. He found it quite uncanny that at 10pm a busy road should be so deserted. God, and it was cold – so damn cold!

After some twenty minutes, he was overwhelmed with relief to find that the light towards which he had been walking belonged to an isolated farmhouse surrounded by a series of dark and dilapidated outbuildings.

He pushed open a gate and cursed as he walked through the quagmire of a yard to the front of the house. The thick slimy mud clammily embraced his ankles and he cursed again as it sank into the tops of his shoes. God only knew what muck he walked through in order to reach the front door. The whole place oozed hostility – or was it simply that he had worked himself into a state? Shaw's natural environment was the city, a world of sophisticated technology. Now, miles away from the support systems of modern life, he was no longer master.

Shaw banged urgently on the door and thought nostalgically of his comfortable house in Blackheath and his wife and daughter. They would be getting ready for bed, but anything could lie ahead for him in this godforsaken place.

"Come on. Come on," he muttered impatiently at the closed door, but it remained shut and he could hear no movement from within. To make matters worse, rain began bucketing down. As he banged more viciously he could feel his self assurance slipping and in its place came a feeling of panic. Then, to his annoyance, the lights inside the house suddenly went out, leaving him in utter blackness.

"Hey! Is anybody there – I need help," he shouted, banging continuously upon the door. "I need a telephone. My car's broken down!"

It soon became clear that whoever was inside had no intention of opening up. He had one more try.

"My name is Robert Shaw," he yelled. "I'm a business man – I mean you no harm. I just need a telephone."

There was no response to his appeal and he realised that he would simply have to take stock of the situation.

"Christ, what a bloody mess," he thought as he swept the torch across the dark muddy yard. If only he could find shelter until morning, that would be something! Then the slim beam of his torch settled on a door belonging to one of the dilapidated outbuildings. The door was slightly ajar!

He picked his way across the rainswept yard, pulled it open and stepped inside. An uncanny stillness enshrouded him. A deep, silent stillness. It felt menacing but at least it was dry, thank God.

He flashed the torch about the building, and quickly realised he was in a barn. It was littered with old farm implements. A huge ancient Fordson Major tractor, complete with faded blue paint and steel seat, slumbered in the corner. On the worm-eaten wooden walls hung horse-harnesses, ladders and great bundles of yellow string. There was a strong smell of stale dust mingled with that of diesel oil. Then he saw the rickety stairs leading to the loft.

Climbing over a horse-drawn plough and through a pile of rotting apple-boxes, he began slowly climbing the stairs. When he reached the loft things started to look more promising. It was less cluttered for a start and an old pallet which stood in the corner covered in potato sacks would do as a bed until morning. At least he'd be protected from the dreadful weather and he certainly didn't fancy the walk back to the car. He would let the night pass and tackle that problem in the morning.

The sacks were surprisingly comfortable. It had been a long and exhausting day and he was grateful just to close his eyes and, he hoped, get a few hours rest.

He had just reached that pleasant twilight world between consciousness and sleep when below the door of the barn slammed shut with such force that he was sure there had been an explosion. He was wide-eyed and alert now as he lay rigid with fear in the darkness. The silence was almost too much to bear, a silence that was no longer empty. Robert Shaw felt that he was not alone. When he heard the heavy footsteps climbing the stairs he knew damn well he wasn't.

His mind worked faster than any computer he had ever sold – but to no avail. He just could not decide what to do. He could hear the footsteps getting nearer and nearer the top of the stairs. A fellow traveller maybe. Someone else had broken down and needed a place for the night. No! Too much of a coincidence. Farm worker on night duty? Thief? Farmer having a last look before bed? Torch, where did I put the bloody torch? Shaw fumbled unsuccessfully for it in the darkness, then froze with fear as a chilling sound assailed his ears, adding fresh horrors to his already reeling imagination. It was the sound of breathing. A loud, wheezing, asthmatic, breathing. Like the footsteps, it grew louder and louder until, unable to bear it any longer Shaw screamed out in terror,

"Who's there? Who are you?"

At the top of the stairs a human form appeared surrounded by an inhuman glow! It was unmistakably a man, an unusually tall and grossly fat man. His clothes were an old-fashioned gentleman's, possibly Edwardian, but there was nothing gentle about this macabre apparition. Puffy flesh gripped a gold monocle and his eyes were staring and demonic.

Shaw shook and whimpered as the huge wheezing form moved slowly towards him on the bed. Too petrified to move, Shaw could do nothing but cringe against the wall.

"Go away," Shaw pleaded, "please go away!"

Then he saw that the apparition was smoking a cigar. Shaw was hypnotised by the cigar and he couldn't take his eyes from it. He no longer looked at the terrifying creature who now stood over him – it was that cigar, that fat glowing cigar! Then the barn was filled with a dreadful roaring guttural laughter which seemed to shake the whole building. Shaw thought he was going insane and clapping his hands over his ears he dared once more to look into the face of the man who stood before him. The demonic eyes bored into him like twin lasers and the huge shoulders heaved in unison. Then he stopped laughing and a look of hatred and contempt spread across his face. Shaw watched in terrifiied fascination as the cigar was now pointed at his face. Before he had time to protect himself, the hideous figure lurched forward and drove the cigar deep into Shaw's cheek. The barn reverberated with his agonised scream. Then he lost consciousness.

When Robert Shaw came round it was dawn and he heard the comforting sound of birds singing and fluttering under the eaves of the barn. He shuddered as he recalled his experience of the night before.

In the pure light of morning it would have seemed logical to attribute the whole incident to a fearful nightmare – logical, that is, except for the deep burn which still seared his cheek. But how could something from non-physical dimension affect human beings?

He raced down the stairs, accross to the house and hammered on the door. This time it opened and a stout ruddy-faced farmer stared impassively at his wounded face.

"He's still around then," said the man without pity or emotion.

"If you're referring to that thing in your loft – yes he is! Something dreadful happened to me in that barn of yours – look at this!" said Shaw aggressively stabbing a finger at the cigar burn.

"You shouldn't 'ave gone up there. Anybody 'round these parts would say the same. He's an evil bugger that one."

"Well, for God's sake man, why didn't you answer your door last night? I only wanted to use your phone."

"We never open the door after dark, sir," the farmer said quietly. "No, we haven't opened that door after dark for many a year."

"That's no consolation to me," said Shaw gently touching the burn on his cheek. "Who the hell is that – thing?"

"Can't tell you that, sir, nobody knows who or what it is." The man turned and called into the house. "Mary, come out here a minute, love."

From behind the door a small woman appeared, wearing an apron. Shaw recoiled in horror as he saw her face. It was covered in scars and there could be no doubt that the wounds had been inflicted by the same cigar which had branded him.

"We learnt a long time ago not to open our door at night, sir. You see, we don't have no trouble with the door closed!"

Seven

The Burglary

Illustrated by Tom Adams

Duncan Avery wore loud clothes and gold glinted at his fingers and wrists. His face, was thin and mean. In fact his only generous aspect was his teeth which were constantly on show.

Avery was a villain. At thirty-eight he had spent a good deal of time inside, for offences ranging from mugging to burglary.

"It's so easy," Avery would say to his equally unsavoury partner, Weasel. "It's like taking candy from a baby."

Avery had all the patter, dress and confidence, Weasel was the technical man. He could case a building, open safes, crack any lock and there was not an alarm system which he could not stifle. They were the perfect team – a marriage of convenience cemented by greed. They neither liked nor disliked each other. Weasel accepted his social limitations, for he, unlike Avery, was stocky, quiet and inarticulate. In bars or pubs when Avery held forth, shooting outrageous lines to gullible, thrill-seeking ears, he would nod on cue and, pointing to his flashy mate, would say supportively.

"He did you know. He bloody did!"

Together they had travelled the length and breadth of England picking choice properties for burglary. All they needed was to find a small, trusting rural community. Then they'd move in and stay for a few days, posing as antique dealers for overseas markets. What Avery and Weasel loved most of all was "working the coast", the South Coast for preference. Here they found the "Costa Geriatrica" whose retired and wealthy inhabitants lived near the sea or in quaint villages a few miles inland. Living soporific lives and largely bored, they were happy to talk and divulge all the information that a clever burglar required. What they didn't reveal in words they did in action. The trusting souls left doors unlocked and garages open as a sign of their absence. It didn't take an expert long, having established that the house was empty, to enter and make off with a haul of valuables. But Avery and Weasel were out of the small time now. They went for the big stuff and planned one good robbery in each town or village.

Every detail would be worked out once the site had been chosen. Each man had a small flat in the East End of London which served as bases to plan their jobs from and somewhere to return to once they had finished. Also they were near fences who would buy their stolen goods.

They first heard about Professor Pritchard's priceless collection of Egyptian ornaments and jewellery in a little country pub in Kent. Using his best Oxford accent, Avery had fallen into conversation with a retired, red-faced Wing Commander. Mellow with pink gin and slurring his syllables, he spoke at length about the old Professor's years in Egypt working as an archeologist.

"If you're in the same business you should have a chat with the old boy," he had said, wrapping his bloodless fingers around a cigarette smoothly offered by Avery. "He's a quiet old bugger but he knows his onions when it comes to Egypt."

Avery allowed his thin lips to slip above and below his huge teeth and beamed that dreadful smile.

"Does he live alone?"

"He does now. Used to have a wife but she kicked the bucket. Cancer, I think. Bloody great house too..."

He looked out of the window and pointed unsteadily. "It's that big white place at the top of the hill." Turning to the bar he ordered another large pink gin. "He must get lonely up there. Lost my wife nine months ago. Bloody awful, loneliness. People don't realise what a bloody awful thing loneliness is."

Avery and Weasel found it a simple matter to case the outside of the house. Inside could have proved more difficult but it didn't. Smoothly dressed, and acting his most oily self, Duncan Avery had walked confidently to the door and pressed the bell.

He was received politely by the old man himself. He explained that he had met Wing Commander Gower and that he had been so delighted to hear of the Professor's collection and had taken it upon himself to call unannounced.

"Are you a dealer?" the benign old gentleman had enquired.

"Yes, but first and foremost a great lover of Egyptian art," had been the smooth reply. As a thief and confidence trickster he had always followed one golden rule and it rarely failed. "Tell them what they want to hear," he would say, "that way you can't go wrong."

Well, it worked like a charm. Delighted to share the beauty of his collection, Professor Pritchard took him on a tour of the house. Avery hadn't a clue about Egyptology but made all the right noises and the old man seemed happy to have the opportunity to talk about his passion.

It was the drawing room which housed the nucleus of the collection and, Philistine though he was, Avery could not help but be impressed by the magnificent array of ornaments. He also noticed the French windows which faced the front garden.

"You will know of course that I was privileged to be the first man to enter the tomb of the Pharaoh Nalhad." said Professor Pritchard, pathetically anxious to communicate. "Most of the objects in this room come from that beautiful place." A dreamy tone of nostalgia had crept into the old man's voice. "The best, of course, are at the British Museum, but I kept a few to remind me of those happy years."

"Wonderful!" said Avery artificially. Then, more cautiously, he asked, "What would they be worth then?"

"How do you put a price on beauty, Mr Avery?" returned Professor

Pritchard. "I've never bothered. I am surprised you haven't asked me about the curse."

Avery twitched. He was being asked to display knowledge he didn't have. Con men don't like that.

"Curse?"

"Come, come, Mr Avery. As a student of Egyptology you've surely heard of the Curse of Nalhad?"

"Oh, yes – the curse, of course. I was so absorbed in these marvellous pieces that I wasn't thinking." Avery glanced nervously at the Professor but he seemed too involved in expounding on his pet subject to notice the gaffe.

The latter breathed a sigh of relief. He'd be more careful in future.

"God knows how I escaped its extraordinary powers. It claimed eighteen lives during the excavation. I often wondered whether the Pharaoh knew I meant no harm to his possessions. I merely wanted to show them to the world. Had I been collecting them for greed — I'm sure I should have died horribly like the others."

He picked up one of a pair of small identical statues. "It is said, Mr Avery, that the Curse of Nalhad is symbolised by these two creatures. Not very pleasant are they?"

Having noted the position of doors, locks and alarms, Avery declined a cup of tea, and, thanking the Professor, left the house.

Later, over egg and chips in a roadside cafe, he outlined his plan to Weasel. No point in hanging about; they'd strike the following night.

"It'll be walk-over," said Avery.

It was a mild night in late October. At midnight Avery and Weasel arrived to find all the lights in Professor Pritchard's house extinguished. Whilst Avery went up to the house, Weasel sat in the getaway car, morosely chewing an apple.

A sporadic wind fidgeted through the trees of the orchard and in the darkness the smell of damp wood and rotten apples mingled with the smoke from Avery's cigarette. He was tense, but feeling at his best. Then, crushing out the smouldering butt with his heel, Avery slipped across the lawn and pressed his body against the side of the house. He took a pair of gloves from his pocket and pulled them on, then slid along the wall until he reached the French windows. Now comes the moment of truth, he thought, for if Weasel hadn't fixed the alarm, he'd had it.

Weasel had been to the house earlier in the day, posing as a representative of the security company, and had assured the old man that a routine check was long overdue and would only take a few minutes. Having successfully killed the system, he left with a smile and a subservient tip of his cap.

Praying that Weasel had done his stuff, Avery slipped the blade of a small penknife between the French windows and, with an audible sigh of relief, flicked the catch. Moving like a cat, he entered the cavernous darkness of the drawing room.

Grinning with anticipation, he flashed his torch over the priceless collection of Egyptian ornaments. As his furtive hands carefully stowed piece after piece in his sack, its beam struck the statues which the Professor had said symbolised the curse. They were no more than three inches high, with the head of a beast which resembled a cross between a lynx and a wolf, and the body of a man. Avery hesitated before placing them in the bag. He left quietly and stealthily, slipping across the garden and back to the waiting car.

In just under two hours Avery and Weasel were back in the East End of London. "Nice tidy little number that, Weasel," Avery said as they parked the car in a hired garage. "I'll see you at the Prince Albert tomorrow night. We'll have a few quid then!"

In his small bedsitter, Avery spilt the contents of the sack onto the bed. The haul was worth more than he could possibly have imagined. To him it was so much junk, but he knew that he could dispose of it for a considerable sum.

The old Professor was heartbroken when he discovered the burglary. It was as if the thief had torn the very guts out of his life. As the police moved about the room hunting for clues the old man shook his head sadly.

"You are wasting your time. He will be dead before you find him!"

When the police asked what he meant by this statement, he repeated, "He will be dead before you find him!"

The fence was staggered by the value of the haul and offered Avery five thousand pounds in cash – a fraction of its true worth.

"Is that all?" asked the thief.

"How much do you think this junk is worth?" asked the fence flatly.

"I don't know."

"Then take the money," said the man with a shrug.

He handed the twin statues back to the thief. "And you can take these as well. I don't want them."

"What's wrong with them. They're old, aren't they?"

"Take them away. I don't want them."

As Avery walked towards the door, the old fence turned his back and muttered, "And God help you!"

"What did you say?"

The seedy-looking receiver shook his head. "It wasn't important. Look, I know where you could get me more of this stuff – interested?"

"Why not?"

"How can I contact you – do you have a name?"

"You'll get a message to me at the Prince Albert. Duncan Avery."

The phone rang in the library and the distraught old man picked it up. His voice was barely audible.

"Professor Pritchard speaking."

The fence disguised his voice. "Professor, I have just purchased the Nalhad collection for ten thousand pounds."

"Dear God, that's wonderful," he said, close to tears. "I never thought I'd see any of it again."

"I knew it had been stolen and you will understand why I have no wish to keep the collection, beautiful as it is."

"I would gladly give you double for its return!"

"Ten thousand pounds will be adequate, Professor. I do not wish to make a profit. I shall return the collection on two conditions. The first is that I am paid in cash and the second is that I remain anonymous."

Professor Pritchard would have consented to virtually anything to ensure the safe return of his collection. "I agree."

"There are two items missing. You will no doubt guess which ones they are?"

"The statues... God help the man who has them."

"I know who he is and can probably find out where he lives."

"They must be found, it is imperative. They are deadly in the hands of strangers. You must tell the police where they are. If you understand the nature of the curse, you will know what I mean. It may already be too late for him!"

"I will give the details when I deliver the collection. I do not wish any personal contact with the police."

"I understand. You have my word."

Avery got violently drunk that night and having paid off Weasel threw his money about childishly. Later he groped his way back to the small dingy room and flung his spent body onto the bed. The drink sent his head spinning and he was forced to splash water into his face in order to check the inevitable nausea. Staggering and swaying, he wiped his face with a greasy towel and then looked into the mirror.

What he saw made his stomach contract and he vomited uncontrollably into the basin. For a moment he thought he was losing his mind. He lifted his head from the basin and with awful terror he once again peered cautiously into the fly-blown mirror. The vile image had not disappeared but had moved closer and the bloodshot eyes of the beast were so paralysing that he was unable to move. Then with a sudden awful realisation he remembered where he had seen the creature before.

"I'll take them back," he screamed. "I'll take them back now, I promise. Just leave me alone. Go away!"

The creature turned him and stared into his petrified eyes. Suddenly, the other beast appeared and began to move towards him. Duncan Avery backed away but they continued to advance. He could feel fetid breath on his face. Avery began to scream hysterically. Then he saw the fangs. Yellow, the saliva boiling amongst them. They came nearer – and nearer. Then he felt the searing pain at his throat.

Following the lead given by the fence, detectives made enquiries at the Prince Albert, posing as friends of Duncan Avery. They soon discovered his address but after knocking many times they had had to break down the door. The two detectives nearly vomited when they discovered the horribly mutilated body caked in dried blood.

Local police eventually returned the two statues to a relieved Professor Pritchard.

"You were right," said the policeman. "He was dead when we found him. Our London colleagues tell us it was one of the most sickening murders they'd ever seen. They found it difficult to believe it was done by a human being. More like an animal."

The old man shook his head. "He was mutilated," he said quietly, "and his throat had been torn to shreds."

"Well yes it had," said the incredulous policeman, "but how did you know that?"

"I was in Egypt a long time, Constable. There are things which are better kept secret."

"I wonder why he kept the statues?"

"He was forced to keep them, Constable. The man to whom the thief sold my collection was a specialist. He too knows about the Curse of Nalhad. I only hope the thief worked alone, for if he had someone helping him with the burglary then God help him. He cannot escape!"

Weasel was shaving for the first time in days. Funny that he hadn't seen Avery for a while. Probably planning the next job. Weasel grinned. Shacked up with some blonde, more like.

Something moved, just outside his range of vision. Then he saw them in the mirror, reflected on either side of his terror-stricken face. Fangs.

Eight

The Nightmare

Illustrated by Bill Donohue

There was a shuffling hush in the courtroom as the jury filed back to the benches. James Wilson stood in the dock visibly trembling. At his side were two policemen, expressionless, ever bored, for they had seen it all before. The judge turned to the foreman of the jury.

"Ladies and gentlemen of the jury, have you reached agreement?"

"We have."

"And what is your verdict?"

"Guilty, your Honour."

Wilson clutched at his chest and slumped forward against the dock.

"Let the prisoner be upstanding," the clerk of the court intoned.

Aided by the two policemen, Wilson stood upright, his eyes fixed on the judge who stared solemnly back at him over his small gold spectacles.

"James Wilson, you have heard the verdict of this jury. You stand convicted and have been found guilty of first degree murder. Is there anything you wish to say before I pass sentence upon you?"

Wilson opened his mouth in an attempt to speak, but no words followed. For the first time in his adult life he was utterly helpless.

"James Christopher Wilson, I sentence you to life imprisonment for the murder of Catherine Amy Stokes. Were it in my power to pass a more severe sentence I should not hesitate for one moment to do so. You brutally and savagely took the life of an innocent young girl whose only crime was that she loved and worshipped you. You have misused the respected office of Mayor with which you were entrusted by your community. You, who should have set a standard of excellence, have slumped to the level of barbarism, committing one of the vilest crimes it has ever been my misfortune to judge. You will, if there is any human feeling in your soul, live with this terrible act for the rest of your life. Take him down."

Wilson had guarded his secret well. He had carried out his civic duties flawlessly and even made a personal appeal on television, requesting information regarding the disappearance of his personal assistant, Catherine Stokes. He had known all the time where she was. Dead. Always a man to take what he wanted, regardless of the effect on others, he had decided exactly what he would do from the moment Catherine came for an interview.

She was nineteen; he was fifty-three. She was embarking on life's adventure, he had already mastered it, having used every trick in the book to secure and increase his personal power within the small Lancashire mining community. It didn't take him long to weave a spell around that naïve creature. With her humble background, how could she resist a life-style she could never have realised existed? It was all there: the chauffeur-driven Rolls; the great man cutting tapes and unveiling plaques. Who was it who said that power was the ultimate aphrodisiac? It certainly worked on Catherine, worked to the extent that she had no life of her own. She became involved in the world of Mayor Wilson to the exclusion of all else. She was his property and he was never slow to capitalise on any available asset – his or anyone else's.

There were the civic functions continuing late into the night. There were, increasingly, private dinners where he introduced her to fine food and champagne. Then came the week-end visits to his holiday cottage and

the stunning reality of first-time physical love. His effect on her was hypnotic, like the power of a snake over its cornered prey. She became a prisoner of love, her mind and body nothing more than an extension of his will. His moods were her moods. His enemies, hers. If he desired something, so did she. Every word he uttered was unquestionably correct. Indeed, she was incapable of either objective thought or independent action.

Then, after six months, during which time he used and enjoyed that young body without scruple, people started to whisper and panic had withered his lust.

Wilson feared scandal above all else. Old associates – for he had no true friends – took pleasure in relating rumours about "Jim and that young lass of his". She, poor thing, was far too innocent to comprehend the devastating effects of a civic scandal, but he knew only too well how many local figureheads would have revelled in his ruin. Who would be the first to send that terse, anonymous note to his wife? Wilson knew he was losing control. She would have to go, and quickly. Suddenly Catherine posed a real threat to his survival.

No matter how Wilson tried to extricate himself from the relationship, the reaction from the girl was one of hysteria. He tried smooth - talking his way out by saying they'd have to cool it off for a while and maybe meet secretly from time to time. But Catherine found it impossible to imagine a life without his love and attention. Seeing her at work became an acute embarrassment to him, for she spent the day in a trance, bursting into tears at the very sight of him. Finally, in desperation, he took a two-week holiday with his wife, leaving instructions that she was to be sacked in his absence. Sacked she was, but it did not aid the plight of Mayor Wilson.

Awaiting him on his return was a small, blue envelope addressed to him in a round, immature hand, a hand he recognised. He tore it open, read the contents and turned white with fear.

"Good God," he muttered to himself, crushing the letter in his fist. "She wouldn't do that to me! She can't do that to me!"

But he couldn't take the risk. What if she did go through with it? What if she did take her life as she threatened if he wouldn't see her again?

What if she left a suicide note naming him as the reason for her desperate act? He was trapped and he knew it. He couldn't afford to go on seeing her, neither could he risk ignoring her. The solution presented itself swiftly to his pragmatic mind. He would have to act and act now.

He went to the phone and dialled the number which she had given in the letter. Catherine answered, her voice soft and vulnerable, the echo of a broken heart. He trotted out platitudes. He sopped her misery with heartily facile words of comfort. They died in her ears like a flame in water. She wanted only one thing.

"Jim, I must see you. I can't go on living unless I see you. Please. *Please.*"

"There, there, lass. Let's go away together. We'll go to the cottage. Next weekend we'll go to the cottage and talk the whole thing through. I'll have to find an excuse, but leave that to me. You get the seven o'clock train on Friday evening and I'll meet you there. How's that suit you?"

Wilson picked up a gleaming new axe at the hardware store and with grim determination set off for the isolated moorland cottage which had been the setting for so many nights of love. He had work to do – hard, physical work – if he was to succeed. He threw himself into that work like a man possessed. By Friday night the preparations were complete. It was a matter now of waiting for the train. She would ring soon and he would pick her up from the station six miles away. If all went to plan it would be the last time she would ever see him or the cottage again. His problem was about to be solved – permanently.

Within an hour of arriving at the cottage with fluttering heart and love-filled eyes, Catherine Stokes was dead. It was the perfect crime. Wilson cleverly concealed the body and scrubbed away every clue which might have suggested that she'd ever been there. He had laboured for over eight hours and, as he burned the suit he had worn for the murder, he felt not one iota of remorse. She was out of his life forever now, and that, after all, had been the object of the exercise.

Later he went to the estate agents to dispose of the cottage without delay. It was, of course, a very desirable week-end residence. An idyllic property in an ideal setting and, at the knock-down price so generously suggested by Mayor Wilson, a quick sale was all but inevitable.

It was the landlord of Catherine's spartan bed-sit who reported her missing, having not seen her for over a week.

Initially he had entered her room more for reasons of rent than compassion. Then he became disturbed when he read the half-finished letter on her table. It was similar to the first letter she had sent to Jim Wilson: the theme was threatened suicide. She had abandoned it as a result of his timely phone call. Assuming Jim to be her young boyfriend, the landlord feared the worst and alerted the local police.

After an exhaustive search throughout the town and the surrounding countryside, a national press and media campaign to find her began. It was during this campaign that a concerned Mayor Wilson appealed to his community for anyone to come forward who could assist the police in tracing the charming young Catherine Stokes. Civic duty done, he watched the weeks slip by and the impetus go out of the search. His plan had worked. They were never going to find the body. The threat had gone and James Wilson was once more in control. Then the cottage was sold.

They were very pleasant people. A professional couple wanting the place as a week-end retreat from the rat race. Wilson showed them around with great charm, lamenting the fact that he couldn't justify keeping the old place on himself.

"Is there a cellar?"

"How remiss of me. Of course. Come this way. As luck would have it I've just decorated."

They loved the cottage and the cellar perfectly suited their purposes. Yes. They would make a decision there and then,

"Delighted, Mr Wilson. We'll take it."

A year passed and with it faded any hope of finding the missing Catherine Stokes. Wilson continued to have the odd bit on the side but, having learned his lesson, never combined business with pleasure again.

Until the nightmare, his horrific act had been a matter of self-preservation. Then, one dreadful night the acid of the past splashed into his sleep and the whole ghastly episode returned to haunt him.

The preceding day had been strange. He had felt unaccountably tense and nervous. His life was as orderly as ever and his affairs smooth and untroubled. Why then did he have this weird sensation that he was being followed? Why did he keep suddenly looking over his shoulder at a presence that wasn't there? Finally, why did he keep hearing his name spoken aloud in places that were totally devoid of people.

That evening, as Wilson tried in vain to concentrate on paperwork, his neck began to prickle with a sensation which was totally alien to him – abject fear. He drank a lot of scotch and roamed the house aimlessly, for he could find no escape from the sense that he was being watched or from the creeping terror that threatened to engulf him. He snapped at his wife when she suggested he should sit down and nor drink so much. She shrugged, packed up her knitting and went to bed.

An hour later Wilson popped two sleeping pills into his mouth and washed them down with the remains of his whisky. He lurched towards the bedroom and, showing no consideration for his sleeping wife, fell heavily into bed. In his restless, drunken sleep he saw no face or figure, but he heard a voice, a voice he would never forget.

"Toss and turn in your sleep, Wilson, you murderer. See the red blazing lights of spilt blood before your closed eyes and know that you are guilty. You who took a life; took it for your own selfish pride and arrogance. Dream, you bastard! Dream and suffer in the blackness of never-ending night for you sent a young soul into that darkness – that darkness in which you now toss and turn in fear.

"Do you remember her? Do you? Do you remember her sweet face before your eyes? Blinding you with her innocence. And what were you but a lying coward ready to take from her, take from her everything that is precious to a woman. She looked at you with trust and revered your experience. She loved you for what you were. Where was your love, Wilson? Where but sunk in the animal appetites and indifference of gross lust. You who had your way and they cast her off like a pair of dirty socks. Never seeing her life; never knowing her mind; never granting her the same divine right to breathe which you so exclusively claimed for your own selfish existence. See the blood on the wall, Wilson, the blood which you spilt.

"Your nightmare is your own creation. You killed her! Cut her down in that lonely cottage for fear that she would tell others of your indiscretion. You silenced her with an axe. Silenced a young soul for fear she would destroy your outwardly decent life. Did you think your wife was blind? Did you think she didn't know about her? You killed in vain, Wilson. Everybody knew and didn't care two damns. So what if you had a grubby affair. Who the hell cares about a man whose ego blinds him to human warmth? But did you have to kill the innocent? Did you have to take her life? Did you have to bury her in concrete to protect your self-contrived reputation? You're sweating and shaking now, locked tightly in the terror that someone will discover her body. Did you know that blood seeps through concrete after a time? It's very distinctive. An expert can tell at once the difference between blood and normal damp.

"You hear a sound in your fearful dream. What is it, Wilson? Now you see the cottage again. Could it be a pick-axe striking a wall? In a cellar perhaps? Who bought the cottage anyway? Do you remember?"

Wilson turned in his sleep and cried out. Momentarily his wife woke, alarmed. Then she closed her eyes again wearily, knowing her husband to be drunk. In Wilson's mind, the voice continued relentlessly.

"People don't like stains, Wilson. They like things clean. The cellar makes an excellent place for wine. The new owners of the cottage are finicky people who earmarked the cellar for it. The trouble is that a stain has marred the perfect white wall and there is an odd smell down there which has grown stronger and stronger over the months. How long ago was it that you sold that little love nest to those city people who were so charmed by your good manners? You see pick-axes tearing into the cement. You see the stain clearly now. They're hacking away at the stained wall and you know it!

"Your wife hears you screaming out in anguish. That same wife that knew about your sordid little fling. She despises you. She's had her own affairs for years. She's glad you're sweating in your sleep. But she knows nothing of the murder, does she? Nothing! They're through, Wilson! The workmen have found the body! One of them had vomited and the other is stunned and unable to stop staring at the tiny form ravaged by decay. Flesh decomposes, Wilson. It putrefies. Moisture seeps through walls; wood will rot. But there is one thing which will die or even change its shape; the one thing, Wilson, of which you are so fond and which so aptly describes your assessment of life. Gold!

"Do you remember the gold locket you gave her? She loved it so, that innocent girl. She never took it off. Neither did you! And it carries something rather special inside, doesn't it? Don't you remember? It carries a portrait of you! A recent photograph of you!"

Wilson crawled out of bed and stumbled to the bathroom. He was shaking from head to foot. The stupid bitch had been wearing that locket – and the axe, he'd buried the axe with the body. Fingerprints, for Christ's sake. Fingerprints! Then he reasoned with himself. He had done the job well. It had been the perfect crime – and he had only been the victim of a nightmare.

Mollified, Wilson returned to bed, having convinced himself that the voice in the nightmare was simply his mind playing tricks.

The following day, at precisely twelve o'clock, the telephone rang.

"Mr Wilson?"

"Speaking."

"It's Ronald Fairbanks here."

"Who?"

"Ronald Fairbanks. I bought your cottage, at Tilburn."

Wilson froze and stabbed the table nervously with a paper-knife. "Yes, yes, I remember," he snapped. "What can I do for you?"

"We've found something here."

"Found something? Found what?"

"A body."

Wilson's mouth went dry and his pulse rate soared. He urged himself to stay cool – to stay in control. "Well, why phone me? It's the police you'll want."

"The police have just left. That's why I'm ringing you."

"I don't understand."

"We discovered the body in the cellar. I keep wine you see and there was this smell, which got worse and worse. Then a dark damp stain appeared on the wall. It got so bad down there that I decided to get it fixed. When we knocked down the wall we found this body. It was the body of a young girl. Horrible! Just horrible!"

"Well, I'm shocked and sorry to hear that, but there's nothing —"

"Well, that's not what the police feel."

"What the hell are you talking about?"

"Don't get angry, Mr Wilson. I'm merely phoning to let you know that they will be calling on you. After all, you were very good to us over the sale and we appreciated it. We know you couldn't have been involved in something as dreadful as this and there's bound to be a perfectly natural explanation for the locket... Just a friendly call so you won't be too surprised when the police pop round."

Visibly shaking now, Wilson clung to the phone and gripped the edge of the table with the other hand with such force that the skin across his knuckles seemed about to split.

"Locket, you say. What locket?"

"A little gold locket. She was wearing it. The police opened it in hope of finding some clue as to her identity. Poor thing, there wasn't much left of her. She'd been dead for quite some time."

"What about the locket?"

"Well, inside it they found a portrait of you in your dress of office. I had to say that I recognised you as the previous owner and where they could contact you. I felt sure you'd want to clear up your side of things. I suppose they've got to do their duty. After all, they've only got the locket and the murder weapon to go on. What animal could have hacked a girl to death like that?" He broke off, muttered a farewell and then rang off.

James Wilson replaced the receiver without replying and stared at the paper knife in his hand. It would be so easy to end his life now. But he couldn't – for he knew that he did not have the courage.

They came for him at three o'clock. During the long days behind bars he suffered not a moment's remorse for the hideous crime he had committed. Instead something else haunted his mind. Dread of the unknown. It was that voice which had first come to him in the nightmare: that voice which now plagued his sleep night after night. Wilson's fear was that when he died there would be someone waiting to greet him. He had the horrifying feeling that it would be the face behind the voice, and from him there would be no escape.

Nine

In a Teacup

Illustrated by Bill Donohue

The stroke was massive, paralysing the left side of William Burchett's body. Fortunately his brain was left undamaged but he literally had to learn to walk and talk all over again.

The stroke was also a great blow to his vanity. He had always played squash and tennis and was quietly proud of his good physique. A man who had grown better looking as he grew older, his silver-white hair, blue eyes and olive colouring still made him very attractive to women.

Burchett was almost back to normal when he was finally discharged from the expensive private clinic. He had been under stress before the stroke, negotiating the sale of his half of a private toy factory, and anyway he was nearing sixty and had no desire to start in business again, so he took the money – close on half a million pounds for his share – sold the London flat and, with his wife Kitty, moved back to the family home in Bristol. She was not terribly practical, preferring to leave to him the responsibilities of running the house, and was forever poking fun at his passion for detail, and on this basis their marriage had been a tolerably comfortable one.

But now, the children either married or living abroad and the house being a large one, the two of them rattled around the place like peas in a can. It wasn't just its size that was getting Burchett down, or the lack of anything constructive to do. He had the strangest feeling that since the stroke something was missing – as if he had been somehow split in two and his other half had deserted him. Logically, of course, it was too ridiculous even to contemplate such a thing but, lying awake in the early hours of the morning with Kitty curled trustingly beside him, it preyed on his mind, making him increasingly moody and short tempered.

At first Kitty tried to joke him out of his bad tempered spells but he turned on her so ferociously that she fell quiet and sad in his presence. She began to stay away for long periods of the day to avoid him. Finally he was totally devastated to find a note stating simply that she had left him for another man.

For days Burchett moped about the house, unable to do anything. Alone for the first time he simply couldn't understand how Kitty could have done such a thing to him. Even if he had been a little grumpy – was this really grounds for her to desert him after thirty years of marriage? Then she telephoned.

They met in a hotel bar. For once she looked pale and serious. He too was nervous. After a few minutes of small talk Burchett snapped:

"Who is he?"

"An artist."

"Christ!"

"He makes me happy. You were making me unhappy. I won't be unhappy. Life's too short..."

"What's his name?"

"Kevin Drummond. He'd like to meet you."

"Never."

"Suit yourself."

"Is he older?"

"Much younger, in fact."

"Has he money?"

"Not a lot. It's not important."

"It's everything. Don't say such damn silly things!"

"If you lose your temper I shall leave. I've told you I won't be made unhappy. He gives to life. What did we ever do but take? It's refreshing to be part of something giving."

Burchett said nothing and after a long silence Kitty touched his hand.

"Money is everything to you. It always was. Remember I've lived with you for over thirty years."

"I never left you short. We were happy enough."

"Only because your indifference allowed me to be myself. When you came out of hospital life became hell on earth and I knew it would never get any better. Then I fell in love..."

"Love! It sounds like madness."

"At least I'm happy."

"I suppose you'll want some of that money you scorn so much – or will you live on laughter and love?"

"I want only a few personal things from the house. As for money, I'll take my chances."

"But damn it woman, you're over fifty – how will you manage?" He drummed his fingers on the table. "Look, contact my solicitor if you ever want anything. You're a bloody fool but I'd never see you go without. You know I still love you."

"Love, William? You don't know the meaning of the word. Take a tip, darling – find out before it's too late." And with that she stood up, kissed him on the cheek and left. With the exception of one brief visit to collect the few items she had requested, he never saw her again.

Burchett was convinced throughout that whole miserable year that at any moment she would appear at the door with her suitcases. He had decided he would play it cool – welcome her in a distant sort of way and then enjoy the miserable details of her flight from reality.

Through those bleak months alone in the huge house, Burchett often thought about their last meeting and Kitty's words. It was true he had only lived for money, but then nothing else, no other possible way of life, made sense or had even occurred to him. He had never thought life anything other than a battlefield on which to survive or be wiped out.

Well, Burchett consoled himself, he had not only survived in material terms, he had triumphed. Although convinced of his personal success, William Burchett began to feel an irritating sense of failure. He had lost his wife and, although he never told her so, she had been the great joy of his life. He realised now that in his scramble for worldly success, she had been his only point of love and happiness. She had reared their now grown-up children and had kept his house ringing with laughter. Alone in bed, during those dreadfully long nights, Burchett became obsessed with a sense of acute inadequacy. He began to think seriously about death and suicide. What had he to live for after all? His children would be delighted to get his money. All their love went to their mother, so again she had triumphed over him.

He had scoffed at her flippant statements, but now they flooded back into his mind and made sense. She believed in a God and she trusted Him. She believed He would look after her and all evidence suggested that He did. It was for this reason that she could walk out of Burchett's life with nothing for she knew that she would be looked after by that unseen hand.

Then Burchett made a decision. He would cut all ties with his past and start a new life. He wanted isolation and to be away from all familiar images of his old habits and haunts. He knew where he would find the solitude he desired. It was in southern Spain, where years ago he had purchased, partly for holidays and partly as an investment, a small villa in the mountain village of Forna. It was the perfect spot, several miles up into the mountains away from the nearest large town of Oliva on the resort coast, lying midway between Alicante and Valencia.

He sold the Bristol house and, with the exception of a special account which he had his solicitor create specifically for Kitty should she ever be in need, transferred his assets to Spain. He took nothing of value from the house, disposing of everything, apart from a few clothes, as he wanted to travel light, to be unencumbered and free of possessions. There was something, however, he did want to take. Kitty's small collection of esoteric books. Perhaps they contained the key which had unlocked the secret door to her happiness.

Having instructed his solicitor that no one was to know of his where-abouts for six months, Burchett travelled to Heathrow and boarded the plane for Alicante. As he awaited take-off, he experienced a strange mixture of emotions. In his stomach he felt a nauseous sense of panic and fear but in his mind he knew there was to be no turning back.

As the plane roared down the tarmac, Kitty's seemingly hard words flashed through his mind:

"Love, William? You don't know the meaning of the word. Take a tip, darling – find out before it's too late."

What on earth did she mean by that?

Although it was late September, the temperature in Alicante was high in the eighties and the airport teemed with exhausted holidaymakers. Burchett viewed them dispassionately. He had always been revolted by humanity in transit, so he collected his bags, picked up the keys to his hired car and moved quickly away from the chaos.

Burchett drove for two hours along the coast to Oliva where he decided to stop and take a drink before winding up the mountain road to Forna, a twenty-minute drive. He knew he had an hour or so before dark and he would need the light to drive up that track to the village. As he walked into the bar he felt dreadfully tired and alone. What in hell's name was he doing with his life?

He had two large whiskies and then set off. Although rough and strewn with hazardous bends, it was a wonderful journey. He remembered going up the track with Kitty chattering and the kids uncontrollably happy at the thought of a holiday. For as far as the eye could see, orange and lemon groves carpeted the valley and were cleverly terraced up the side of the mountains. Towering above the entrance to the village a yellow cube-shaped Moorish castle stood chillingly bleak against the blood-red sunset. Why had he always hated that castle so? Why had he always refused to join Kitty and the kids when they had trekked up the mountainside to walk around its decaying walls and spook each other in the dungeons? He loathed and resented its presence. To him it was evil, yet he could never understand why. To make matters worse it was directly in line with the view from his patio, where he tried to avoid looking at it, doing so only by accident. The worst torture he could possibly imagine was to be alone in that place.

Burchett drove along the narrow road through the village and turned left at the little building which housed the communal well. From here it was a short drive up a steep track to his villa. His was one of a small group of modern Spanish style dwellings clinging to the side of the mountain. In the winter about sixty people stayed in Forna and many of these were British expatriates who had opted out of the rat-race and settled for its immense tranquillity. There, time stood still. Days meant nothing. Sunshine bathed the village all year round and life was inexpensive and totally undemanding. Indeed activity, apart from socialising in an unhurried way, was avoided. This was the land of tomorrow – a place to be, not to do. The name of the game for the expatriates was lotus-eating and they seemed, on the surface at least, to love every minute of it. To add to its attraction, the Spanish inhabitants lived in friendship and harmony with the newcomers. Forna was, as the Spaniards continually reminded themselves and others, all about "Tranquilo" – happiness and harmony.

Burchett parked the car and let himself in. He was pleased to see that their old maidservant, Rosita, had received his message and had tidied the villa, made beds and put cold meat and salad in the fridge. She had been doing this for years and Burchett paid virtually nothing for her kindness. As a businessman he had never been able to understand the villagers' enormous warmth and generosity. It was hard to give them anything since their joy was in giving not taking. Kitty loved and understood them perfectly, and they had idolised her for it. Yes, the Spanish understood love and human warmth. Perhaps it sprang from their years of poverty. They were richer now but they had not yet lost the joy of giving.

For the first four days he did the usual rounds. He met old friends and acquaintances, explained away Kitty's absence and revealed very little about his plans. Most days he ate at one of the two bars and when he felt sufficiently settled, told the regulars that he was locking himself away to work on a thesis. He knew they would leave him alone – that was part of the deal in Forna, "tranquilo".

In the deep silence of the village Burchett began his study of alternative thinking. He began to read Kitty's books on ancient religions, primitive customs, evolution and philosophy. He threw himself into the spiritual sciences like a man possessed.

Only leaving the villa for an odd meal from time to time, Burchett began to look tired and haunted. It was not working. The more he read the more confused and agitated he became. Nothing made sense. Buddhism, Hinduism, Zen; even Christ, the pivot of Christianity, had no revelation or reality for him. It did not move or inspire him to anything but frustration. It was a load of impractical rubbish from which nothing could be gained. The world was as it appeared. There were no other dimensions. No spiritual revelations. No God if He cannot be seen. No extraordinary powers to cultivate or call upon. Darwin was right, life generated and shaped itself. Who cared how – nobody would ever be able to answer that so why bother asking the question. Why had he become so ashamed of his wordly abilities? They were real at least. One created and built and one profited. That was the order of life. Was there any damn profit in words of elusive wisdom. To think he'd sold a perfectly good house and burnt his boats simply to read this trash.

Eventually, Burchett decided that it was Kitty's departure that had forced him into this senseless blunder. She had unhinged his mind, so that he couldn't think clearly any more. Damn her, why did she have to leave?

"At least while I'm in this bloody place I can take a holiday!" And so saying he stamped out of the house into the nearest bar.

"How's the thesis going, William?" asked a comfortably rotund and tanned Welshman.

"Finished."

"Happy with it?"

"Happy as I'll ever be."

The bar was horrendously noisy, since it was lunchtime and lines of tables groaned under the wine and food of fieldworkers from the groves. Glasses were banged with delight onto the tabletops and although merely talking the labourers sounded as if they were threatening to slaughter each other. Burchett had forgotten the Spaniards' love of noise. It was a sensual delight to them, a symbol of life.

He walked over to a group of Englishmen and their wives seated at a table in the corner.

"May I join you?"

"Of course, dear boy," said Captain Williams, pointing politely to a spare seat. "You know everybody, of course, except I don't believe you've met Dorothy Milton, a newcomer to the village."

"William Burchett. How do you do."

They shook hands and he sat down. It was a pleasant feeling to be among his own people again and he was relieved that he'd packed in his ridiculous quest for self-knowledge. This was reality, thank God!

"How long are you staying this time, William?" someone asked from the end of the table.

"Long enough to sell up. I shan't need the place now that the kids are grown and you know about Kitty..."

"Yes, poor show that," said Captain Williams, self-consciously knocking out his pipe.

"I'm looking for a property round here myself, Mr Burchett," said Dorothy Milton. "I'd be very interested to see whether yours would suit me or not."

"You're very welcome to look, whenever you wish."

"It might be perfect for you, Dorothy," brayed Captain Williams' portly wife, who was being constantly tugged by a skinny white French poodle. "You must know the place, it's just above us on the right."

"When will it be convenient for me to view the villa, Mr Burchett?" asked Dorothy Milton.

"Why don't you come and have tea this afternoon. Any time, just stroll up. I'll be there."

"Shall we say about three-thirty then?"

He raised his glass in agreement and as he did so he noticed her eyes for the first time. They were an extraordinary dark brown, full of depth and intensity. She reminded him of somebody, not physically, but in a general atmospheric way, and she seemed totally relaxed and self composed. He imagined her to be a widow, perhaps in her late fifties. He looked at her for a while and she returned his gaze. Then he knew: Kitty, of course, she reminded him of Kitty.

Dorothy Milton arrived on the dot of three-thirty and noted that he had made a special effort over tea. A table had been set on the patio with good china and a small plateful of teacakes. It was a beautiful day and the village luxuriated peacefully beneath a blue cloudless sky. Not a sound

could be heard. It was as if the mountains defied anyone to disturb their long and ancient slumber.

Burchett showed her around the villa and at the end of the tour she was quite frank with him.

"It's too big, I'm afraid. I'm on my own now – rather like you I gather." She sat down at the table and rested her hands comfortably in her lap. "My husband died last year, Mr Burchett."

"I wish you'd call me William."

"Thank you. You see, I want something small to retire to. I've got a certain amount of money, William, but not much. I can live comfortably here but not in England."

"Won't you miss England?"

"Probably, but only sentimentally and I'll get over that in time. It's the same planet after all. Only fear makes us seek the familiar – don't you agree?"

"I've never really thought about it. Do you like Earl Grey?"

"Oh yes, that will be a real treat. I'm sick of tea bags. Can you buy it over here?"

"I bring it with me. I'm afraid this teapot's a bit ancient and I haven't got a strainer. Hope you don't mind a few tea leaves?"

"As a matter of fact I adore them."

"How can you adore tea leaves?" He laughed at her indulgently.

"Believe me, I do."

They sat comfortably together in the warm sunshine and drank the tea. He politely offered a teacake and, although she loathed them, she took one out of consideration for his thoughtfulness.

When Burchett saw that Dorothy had finished her tea he asked her if she'd like another.

"No, thank you, but may I look into your teacup?"

"Whatever for?"

"Just a bit of fun. I read tea leaves, you see. I told you I adored them. May I?"

She took the cup and turned it around in her hand. "How very strange," she muttered to herself.

"What is it?" asked Burchett.

"These leaves, I've never known them speak so clearly. You must be careful. There," she said, pointing into the cup, "you can see a small accident." Then she added as she studied the leaves more closely, "It may leave a scar." She fell silent for a while and seemed to become entranced.

"I'm intrigued," said Burchett, leaning over to look at what was to him a jumble of tea leaves at the bottom of a cup. "But you can't really expect me to believe in this rubbish."

But she did not respond and he became uncomfortable when he saw the strange expression on her face. Then, Dorothy Milton pulled her gaze away from the cup and fixed him with those intense brown eyes. Her voice was slow but very positive. It was also quite different in tone.

"If you wish to survive, you must leave Forna. You are in imminent danger of dying unless you do."

"Oh, what rubbish – you sound just like Kitty."

"Please, take me seriously. I've never been wrong. I can see a building. It stands high up on a hill – even higher! If you ever go there you will die."

She suddenly shook her head and put down the cup. "That was strange. I can't get the hang of this mediumship. It's only just started happening to me. One minute I'm here and then I can't remember anything more. I remember telling you to beware of an accident but I don't remember anything after that... I hope I gave you good news from the other side?"

"Other side," said Burchett angrily. "There is no other side. Life is here and now and I'm sick of all this clap-trap which pretends otherwise."

"Then I feel very, very sorry for you. Thank you for the tea and for showing me the villa. I must be going now."

She shook his hand and left.

Burchett regretted his outburst for he'd enjoyed her company. As he picked up the tea tray he made the mistake of looking straight ahead. On the top of the mountain across the valley the desolate decaying castle looked back at him like a monster crouched ready to spring. He felt the hairs on the back of his neck stand up and he shivered despite the heat.

"Damn that place," he muttered, and his words were sucked into the silence of the mountains.

For the next few days, Burchett thought very seriously about what he was to do with his life, finally deciding to return to England and probably buy a small cottage in the country. Living amidst the beauty of Forna he had never felt so alone. He dreaded the nights more than any other time, for when he fell asleep he was besieged by nightmares, and, when he lay awake in the dark, his mind raced off at weird tangents. He hated the unreality of it all for it seemed that he was constantly attacking himself when alone – as if he needed to hate himself, to punish himself. But for what? He would think most of the day about the fantasies of the night. But why was he suddenly full of fear and uncertainty? Why, after years of good solid reasoning had his mind become an enemy to torment him whereas before it had always been a controlled and logical tool.

Into his nightmares returned that awful sense of incompleteness and he was chasing his missing half through the silent corridors of his dreams, to stay with him during the day until it was bordering on obsession.

After yet another sleepless night, Burchett decided that hard physical work was the answer to his frame of mind. There were tiles that needed fixing on the roof and he knew he should attend to them before any one else came to see the place. But as he was carrying a ladder up the stairs, on his way to the roof, Burchett lost his footing and crashed to the ground smashing his face onto the ladder as he fell. The gash was deep and he was taken to Oliva where the doctor put seven stitches into the wound above his eye. He remembered Dorothy Milton's prediction for there was no doubt he would be scarred. Burchett froze, for if this had come true then what about her warning of imminent death?

Finally he convinced himself that the whole affair must be a coincidence. Yet he still couldn't understand why the castle disturbed him so much. Surely that was imagination. She had told him in her trance to avoid a large building on a hill or higher – was she referring to that place as well? Maybe she had read his mind for he believed that this, at least, was possible.

Then, for his own pride and peace of mind, Burchett decided there was only one thing to do. He would confront his fears once and for all. He would climb that mountain track and he would spend the whole night in that God forsaken place. Tonight, he would do it – tonight! He gazed

at the castle and once again it stared knowingly back at him.

At sunset, Burchett put bread, cheese and a bottle of brandy into a bag, walked through the village and began climbing up the well-worn track leading to the castle. It was not a long climb and within ten minutes he was standing outside the huge, open wooden doors. It was at this moment that he was overwhelmed by the greatest fear he had ever known. Darkness gathered as he walked through the door and into the jungle of grass and weeds which had once been the courtyard. All the rooms were built into the huge thick walls, and only a few of these were in any condition to enter. He stumbled over loose masonry and entered a long dark room on the right which had a further small circular room attached at the end. Every nerve in his body vibrated. There was evidence of the hippies who had once occupied it until the police removed them. Old boots, magazines and rotten blankets littered the floor. The silence was agonising. William Burchett was testing his faith in reality but he felt as though he had walked into the white-hot teeth of hell. He felt a sense of evil stifling his very breathing.

Finally Burchett settled into a curve of the circular room. The hours passed and the moon shone from a great hole in the roof offering some comfort in that hideous nightmare of nothingness. He crouched in the dark, huddled like a man slowly freezing to death. He was alone. So very much alone. Then something strange happened.

Burchett began to see his past life unfold before him. It was like sitting in a cinema, watching a film of which he was the star. It showed every detail of where he had been and what he had done. He saw his children growing up with Kitty and himself watching them – detached, isolated from their joy. He realised that he'd never really known his own children and now he had a sudden longing to hug and kiss them. Tears welled in his eyes as he saw Kitty flitting about the house, laughing. God how he'd loved her – why had he never told her so? The visions ceased and he felt the pain as the ladder hit him. Burchett wiped the tears from his eye and touched the wound, feeling strangely reassured that it was there. Reflecting on his life he knew he had failed either to give love or to receive it with generosity. It really didn't amount to very much in the end.

Suddenly Burchett stiffened with fear. He heard footsteps, but could see nothing. Then a shaft of moonlight fell upon the approaching figure, illuminating it like a stage spotlight. Burchett stood up and pinned himself against the wall. The great silence of night echoed with his screams as the man walked towards him, arms outstretched as if to embrace an old friend. But it was no ordinary man who stood before William Burchett, it was himself, right to the stitches he still carried above his eye.

William Burchett had found his missing half. He watched, horror-struck, as their two bodies merged, and for a single shattering moment he experienced all the sensations that passed through them both. Then he was seized again by the stroke that had once so nearly killed him, and slumped to the floor.

Days later, children playing in the ruins discovered the body. Only one. The other had returned to that world in which William Burchett had tried so hard to believe. He had found his soul, but in so doing paid the ultimate price.

Ten

The Oil Rig

Illustrated by Graham Humphries

Grey freezing waters surged and thrashed at the huge oil rig, which stood like a vulnerable pylon in the sea. Looking at it through the windows of the helicopter, McAlistair shook his head incredulously, for it never ceased to amaze him just what modern man could do when faced with the promise of profit. Yet he felt secretly glad to be part of that achievement. He was also delighted that he was able to apply his diving skills so close to home and to reap the considerable financial rewards which went with the job.

Before the advent of North Sea oil, Andrew McAlistair had been obliged to travel all over the world in order to reap the highest rewards for his skills. Diving to great depths in the angry waters off the coast of Scotland was certainly hazardous but at least, unlike working in the Persian Gulf, he was able to see his family on a regular basis. All in all life was good to him. "Grab it while you can!" was the general attitude of the crew who staffed the rigs. They were hard men, working for top wages in

a unique environment which they knew could not last forever. The hazardous and alien conditions under which they lived and laboured created an atmosphere of unspoken excitement.

Then the helicopter's human cargo was landed on the semi-submersible drilling rig where they would work, sleep, eat and spend their recreation periods for the next few weeks.

McAlistair's first task was to prepare himself for a routine under-water inspection of the structure. He entered the small diving bell with a colleague, Bill Frobisher, and very soon they were lowered into the heaving water. Below the surface all was dark and still as the bell began its descent to the bottom hundreds of feet below. It was not a deep dive and very soon the bell was suspended a few yards above the sea-bed.

Since it was his turn to make the inspection, McAlistair went through a final safety check. Then, hooking his life line onto the heavy diving suit, he signalled to Frobisher and slipped out through the bottom of the bell. He glided, half walking, half floating, towards the sub-sea wellhead. For some time he glided around, flashing a powerful torch over the precious wellhead that pierced the ocean bed like a giant hypodermic from the rig above. He had all but completed the inspection when he was overcome by a strong feeling that he had been in that precise spot before. And at a time when the rig hadn't even been imagined. It made no sense at all.

As McAlistair prepared to return to the bell, he saw something out of the corner of his eye which made him turn, then go rigid with shock, for standing only feet from him was the ghostly figure of a man. It glowed phosphorescently in the dark water and seemed to wear an old fashioned sea captain's uniform. The figure beckoned McAlistair to follow it and pointed in a direction a few feet left of where he stood. McAlistair's first impulse was to go like hell for the safety of the diving bell, but then he realised that he felt no great fear or threat from the ghostly form. He headed towards it and as he did so, the figure seemed to dissolve then disappeared altogether.

Circling his torch McAlistair spotted the remains of an old wreck. He entered it through a huge gaping hole in the hull. There was little left of the ship's interior, but as he probed around McAlistair saw the remains of a cabin and resting on a rotten table he saw a small lead casket. McAlistair picked it up. As he was leaving the wreck the ghostly figure appeared again and seemed to smile at him. He should have been terrified but to his surprise he felt merely intrigued.

Safely back on the rig, McAlistair and Frobisher, surrounded by an inquisitive group of onlookers, bent over the lead casket. McAlistair felt a tremendous excitement coursing his veins and an Englishman laughed,

"Trust a bloody Scotsman to find the treasure. Open it up, man!"

McAlistair tried in vain to turn the key which was still in the lock, but it wouldn't budge. The casket was passed around the group and each man attempted to turn the key but without success.

"I'll get some pliers, Jock," shouted somebody.

"No," said McAlistair sternly. "I'm not going to force it. Anyway the key might snap."

"What about heating it," said another.

"It's lead – you'll fuse the lock."

"Then what are you going to do with it, Jock?"

"I don't know... I'll think about it later." He turned to Frobisher. "Whatever's inside we share, okay?"

Frobisher made a gesture of refusal. "You found it, mate. It's yours."

"No, it's ours and we share. Let's get out of these suits and get some food. We'll try again later."

It was November, a time when the sea could be at its most treacherous and, on the night of the twenty-first, it lived up to its reputation. A storm had blown up suddenly and by midnight, air-sea rescue teams were put on alert and company helicopters stood by to ferry the crew to safety. Winds of up to a hundred miles an hour howled round the rig and forty foot waves thrashed its lanky structure. Even the hardered oilmen were afraid. Later, these fears were intensified when rumour spread that the rig, a semi-submersible structure, was drifting.

The first of the rescue helicopters began arriving at midnight and non-essential members of the crew were shuttled back to the mainland. Overhead an RAF Nimrod circled, keeping a constant watch on the situation below. Conditions had become critical.

Andrew McAlistair was considered important enough to have to stay behind. Alone in his quarters he viewed the situation seriously enough to write a just-in-case letter to his wife saying goodbye and giving her details of his financial affairs should he not survive. When he had finished the letter he felt rather stupid. After all, he'd been in storms before. This was a bad one, and yes, the rig was drifting, but it could be effectively anchored, and the storm would pass.

In the frenzy and confusion created by the storm, McAlistair had completely forgotten about the casket. Now, as he settled down for what looked certain to be a sleepless night, he picked it up and examined it again. For fear of masculine ridicule he had decided against telling anyone how he had found it or about the ghost of the captain that he had seen. He tried opening it again but it remained fast. In the end he decided that he would take it ashore on his next leave and get it opened by a professional locksmith.

He placed the casket on a bedside table beside a photograph of his wife and children and got ready for bed. There was no point in removing the bulk of his clothes for he knew, with conditions as they were, that he could be called for emergency duty at any moment. Picking up a well thumbed and circulated paperback, McAlistair climbed into bed, covered himself with a duvet, and began to read. He thought at first that it was the immense force of the wind gusting through the rig that created the sound which bore uncanny similarity to human screams of fear and confusion. He put down the book and listened more intently. It was as if he had had a mild electric shock, for above the wind he heard a deep, distinct voice yell that final order feared by all seamen. "Abandon ship! Abandon ship!"

He leapt from his bed, raced to the cabin window and looked out to sea. He found himself staring, incredulous, at the ghostly silhouette of an old sailing ship slowly slipping beneath the boiling waves. The screams of the terrified crew rang in his ears. Within a few seconds the ship had disappeared and the awful cries of anguish were stilled. Unable to watch the terrifying emptiness of the sea any longer, McAlistair turned violently from the window, sweeping the lead casket from the table as he did so.

He left his cabin and walked the few yards along the corridor to Frobisher's room. It was two o'clock in the morning, and he tapped very

gently on the door. Frobisher, unable to sleep because of the storm, opened the door immediately. He, too, was still dressed and a half-finished bottle of whisky described how he had decided to pass the night.

"For medicinal purposes," he said, with a wink. "There'll be precious little sleep tonight. Did you hear the forecast?"

"Only the earlier one..."

"Supposed to be improving. Should be clearing up soon. Och, but I never put faith in those buggers! Will you have water in your whisky?"

"Did you hear or see anything strange tonight?" asked McAlistair, feigning a matter of fact tone.

"Strange?"

"Aye, strange! Noises, like screaming men, coming from the sea?"

"Have you been drinking already? There's only one sound coming from out there tonight and that's the sound of this bloody storm!"

"I saw something out there tonight. An old wooden sailing ship sink, and I heard the crew screaming as they abandoned ship. I saw it and I heard the voices."

"Are you having me on or something? Maybe you've got cabin fever – Christ I get sick of this place after a month."

"I didn't tell you how I found the casket yesterday. I thought you and the lads would laugh me out. You see, I saw a ghost down there..."

"A water ghost, that's original!"

"I'm serious, Bill. I saw a ghost. He was an old fashioned sea captain and he showed me where the wreck was. That's how I found the casket."

"You're off your head, man!"

"I'm telling you what I saw. I don't expect you to believe me. Before yesterday I would have laughed too." He took a mouthful of scotch and paced the room. "It was all so real. I saw the ship as clearly as I see you."

"Och, have another drink. They say strange things happen at sea, but that story's cracked, man. Did you have any luck with the casket? I'd love to know what's inside."

"No, I thought I'd wait until we go ashore, and get a locksmith to open it. Pity to force it."

"I wouldn't have the patience to wait. It's probably that old ghost's spittoon... Perhaps that's why he's still hanging around. He's maybe waiting for a laugh when he sees the expression on your face when you open it.''

The two men sat drinking and talking together without thought of time. Eventually McAlistair walked over to the window and drew back the curtain.

"Have you noticed anything different?"

"Different?"

"Aye, you drunken swine, the storm's died down."

"Thank God for that! We can maybe get some sleep now. That was a bad bugger. The worst I've ever seen!"

"I was a wee bit worried myself for a while there. I even wrote a farewell letter to Mary and the kids. I had a funny feeling we weren't going to make it. Sounds stupid now, but seeing that ghost ship was like glimpsing my own death."

"You really did see something didn't you?"

"Bill, I swear to God I saw it." He drained the last drops of whisky from his glass. "Who knows, maybe someone else did too."

"Maybe. Ye Gods man, look at the time, it's past four. I'm to my bunk. There will be plenty to do tomorrow after this little lot."

McAlistair thanked him for the drink and returned to his cabin. He felt totally exhausted as he climbed into bed and the sweet thought of sleep comfortably enveloped his somewhat jumbled mind. He vaguely recalled the strange things that had taken place, the old sea captain, the ghost ship and the casket which now lay on the floor beside his bed. Within minutes he fell into a deep, troubled sleep.

McAlistair stubbed his foot on the casket as he climbed out of bed that morning. Then he saw that the key had snapped, somehow managing to trigger the locking mechanism so that the lid was partly open. He grabbed the box excitedly and, opening it, gazed down at the contents – an old but well preserved log book. Gently, he removed the book and began flicking through the pages. Recorded in a small, meticulous hand were the day to day events of life on the clipper *Lady Jane* as she journeyed around the British coastline in the early 1780s. He suddenly had a fleeting but intense picture of the ghost ship. McAlistair turned to the last entry and read with incredulity:

Captain's Log, November 22nd, 1782. 7am.

The fierce storm of yesterday finally abated during the night, thank God, it being some of the worst weather ever encountered by this crew and vessel. I am afeared that more is to follow for as I write I look through my cabin window and can see a great black rolling mountain of cloud. In my entire experience of the sea, I have never seen anything of the like. If it be a storm, then God help us all, for it looks as if it carries the very Devil himself.

It was signed, *Daniel Williamson, Captain of the* Lady Jane.

Andrew McAlistair felt suddenly uneasy. Something nagged at his mind. Something he had read in the entry niggled at him so that he read it again and again. Then the sound of those screaming men abandoning ship the night before came flooding back. And that strange old sea captain. Fantastic events but what, if anything, did it all mean? There had to be a logical connection between the wreck on the bottom from which he'd taken the casket, and the ghostly one he had seen go down. But it was clear from the last entry in the log that they had survived a violent storm but were still threatened by greater danger. Perhaps they didn't make it.

Then it struck him like a thunderbolt and he was overwhelmed by a mixture of horror and disbelief. What had been eluding him in that final entry suddenly became clear; the date, November 22nd, 1782. Two hundred years to the day.

He moved slowly and fearfully to the window and looked out to sea. His body seemed to sag under the pressure of an unseen weight. In the distance a mountainous cloud of impenetrable black was coming towards the rig, looking for all the world as if it held the very Devil himself!

Eleven

The Ghostwriter

Illustrated by Tom Adams

He sat at the end of the airy bar, turning an ice-cold glass of lager aimlessly in circles. The classic English country inn was the perfect antidote to the intolerable pressures he had suffered for nearly a year, for labouring over the last three chapters of a novel, his imagination had gone stale and his daily output reduced to a trickle.

Lionel Turner had begun to fear what writers dread most: the terrifying prospect of drying up – a creative block. Staring at blank sheets of paper with a deadline hanging over him like some awful bird of prey, he had taken his agent's advice to leave London for a while. Now, surrounded by oak beams, horse brasses, ingle-nook fireplaces, the smell of polish and the promise of utter peace, Lionel felt a little more at ease.

The landlord had given him a choice of rooms as the season had ended and the writer was his only guest. Lionel had chosen a small cosy attic at the rear of the pub with a view across an undulating Kent valley in the magnificent throes of autumn.

Now Lionel Turner sat savouring his beer and feeling relaxed for the first time in months. There would be no cronies here to entice him to have that other drink or drag him to those interminable parties that he so abhorred. For no particular reason, he picked up his glass and wandered into the adjoining bar. The room was quiet and empty and he sat down at a table in front of a window which commanded the same glorious view as he enjoyed from his bedroom. A marvellous tranquility enveloped him as he watched the dying sun cast a soft pink blanket over the mellow autumn day.

Then his peace was punctured by sheer disbelief. The ashtray suddenly slid across the tabletop and crashed to the floor. Lionel stared at the object. He hadn't jolted the table and he certainly hadn't touched the ashtray, so what the hell had made it move so violently? He picked it up and put it back on the table.

He watched in amazement and a little fear as it once again slid across the polished wood and landed on the floor. The process was repeated a couple more times until Lionel smiled, concluding that he was the victim of some practical joke perpetrated on newcomers to the Rose and Crown.

Leaving the ashtray on the floor he decided to phone his wife Lana and then go to bed early. He was missing her already, and the children, but until he had this block licked he knew he wouldn't be fit to live with. Putting his empty glass down on the bar with a grin, Lionel said to the publican, "I like your flying ashtray."

"Flying ashtray?" replied his surprised host. "I'm afraid I don't follow you, sir."

"Oh, come on. The ashtray sliding off the table. How do you do it?"

The publican cocked a suspicious eyebrow at him and leaned heavily across the bar.

"I really don't know what you mean, sir. What ashtray?"

Lionel began to feel slightly stupid for the man obviously hadn't a clue what he was talking about.

"Are you seriously telling me it's not a joke?"

The resigned shrug of the publican's shoulders and his bemused expression convinced Lionel that he was giving his host the impression that he was slightly eccentric.

"Watch this!" Lionel said, and returning to the ashtray he picked it up and put it back on the tabletop. The publican stood on tiptoe to get a better look, although nothing interrupted his view of the ashtray which remained perfectly still. Lionel had the air of a magician as he willed it to move, and the publican, still on his toes, waited patiently for something to happen. The situation was rapidly becoming farcical.

"But it's not moving..."

"No, sir, it's not moving."

"But that ashtray slid off that table at least twice and I never touched it." Lionel stared at the landlord incredulously. "I really thought you were playing a joke on me." His voice trailed unhappily away and, mumbling an excuse, he walked self-consciously over to the telephone.

He had called his family, unpacked his manuscript for the morning and gone to bed exhausted, pushing the incident of the ashtray from his mind. But now, lying in the darkness, he relived the whole episode. There simply was no explanation, yet he had seen the ashtray move. His thoughts wandered towards the possibility of a poltergeist and he felt oddly comforted by the idea that he may have actually witnessed a genuine paranormal phenomenon.

Too tired to think, Lionel drifted toward sleep. Then he was instantly re-awakened by an odd, rattling sound. Lying rigid in the darkness, Lionel prickled with fear. Was it the sash banging? No. The window was steel-framed, shut and leaded, and anyway it had been a still evening. The door perhaps; could it be the door? He strained his ears, trying to work out which direction the sound was coming from. No, it was more central, far more central. His imagination ran wild with horrifying visions. The rattling increased in intensity and he suppressed a childish impulse to bury himself under the bedclothes. Oh, what he'd give now for a few London parties and a room bursting with music and laughter. Lionel Turner was terrified.

Then, unable to stand the suspense any longer, he sat bolt upright in bed and switched on the bedside lamp. Lionel simply could not believe his eyes when he saw what was causing the sound – his own fountain pen, gyrating like a mechanical toy beside the typewriter. Slowly, heart thumping like a kettle-drum, he climbed out of bed and advanced to-

wards the table. Every nerve in his body tingled as he picked up the vibrating object.

Lionel held the pen for a moment and then felt his hand drawn to a sheet of paper. Copper-plate handwriting began to flow over the page and the words appeared, *"Chapter Nine"*. Lionel then felt himself forced into a chair and, unable to resist, he wrote for some time.

When he finally began to read what he had written, or rather transcribed, he was astonished. It was clearly part of a novel, but by whom, for he was reading about characters that he had never invented, woven into a plot which he had not structured. The style was slightly old-fashioned but the writer was professional and very competent.

Exhausted now, Lionel went back to bed and slept till morning. He did not mention the experience to anyone and throughout the next day he worked at his own manuscript, though with little result.

When the evening came he once again sat alone in the small darkened bar. He wondered whether or not he should phone Lana and tell her about the whole thing, but decided against it for some instinct told him that this was something he had to solve on his own. Then Lionel felt a light touch on his shoulder. He turned but there was no-one there. He felt compelled to return to his room.

The pen on the desk rattled and spun as he entered and again he felt the light touch on his shoulder. Taking up the pen, Lionel sat down and began to write. The work held him for nearly four hours and when, utterly spent, he put down the last full stop, he knew the novel was complete. It was only the next day when, re-reading what he had penned, that he noticed a note on the bottom of the manuscript. *"Title of book – JULIET. Please deliver to Messrs Grantham and Wills of Fleet Street, London."* It was signed *"With thanks, Lindsay Ellis."*

The name seemed familiar. Lionel went downstairs to the phone and, having got the number of the Fleet Street publisher from Directory Enquiries, dialled and asked to speak to somebody connected with fiction who might know of a writer called Lindsay Ellis.

There was a short pause during which Lionel considered his bizarre position. If Lindsay Ellis was known to the publisher, how on earth was he to explain how he had come by the last chapters of his book. He did not

want to admit the extraordinary circumstances under which he himself had penned those final pages. He knew that to do so would put him at the mercy of copy-hungry critics carping about "publicity stunts scraping the slimy barrel of credibility". They would cynically assume that the Lindsay Ellis affair was a cheap and decidedly suspect way for him to publicise his own forthcoming novel. He shuddered as he envisaged the reviews: "In his latest work, automatic writer, Lionel Turner, indeed shows all the characteristics of a first class automaton. His prose, sterile and mechanical."

"Bob Barrington. Can I help you?"

"Are you familiar with the name Lindsay Ellis?"

"Very much so, we published him for many years."

Lionel felt suddenly cold.

"You say you *did* publish him?"

"Yes, he's been dead for over ten years now. His books are still available from libraries, of course."

Lionel took a deep breath. "What would you say if I told you I had in my possession the last five chapters of his novel *Juliet?*"

"That it's impossible. He died before completing the book."

"Are you sure?"

"Absolutely. Lindsay was a close friend of mine. I edited his work for over fifteen years. Tell me, how did you know about *Juliet?*"

Lionel thought rapidly for a moment before replying to the question. Was there really any point in trying to explain what had happened in that little attic room?

"Let's just say the chapters were presented to me. I'll send them to you."

"It's really quite uncanny," said the editor. "Lindsay had planned thirteen chapters for *Juliet* and we have the first eight. Won't you give me the details? It was definitely to be his greatest work. I simply cannot believe that he completed it before he died."

"Could he have done so without your knowing?"

"Well, yes, I suppose it's just possible. Unlikely but possible."

"Tell me, did Lindsay Ellis type his work or use longhand?"

"Oh, definitely longhand. A most distinctive copper-plate style."

Lionel was silent for a moment. Then, slowly, "Mr. Barrington..."

"Yes?"

"Where did Lindsay Ellis die?"

"Well..."

Lionel could feel Barrington hesitate.

"Is it really relevant?"

"Yes. I think it is." Lionel could feel his heart racing and his hand shook as he clasped the telephone receiver.

"Then..."

"Where did Lindsay Ellis die, Mr Barrington?"

"He died in the country. In an old pub. He was suffering from a writing block and I'd suggested he isolated himself from everyone in an attempt to get rid of it." Barrington paused. "He had a heart attack. The landlord found him in the attic room where he had been working, but it was too late."

As Lionel hung up he felt someone pat him gratefully on the back.

Once in his room, Lionel Turner decided to write a short story; a limbering-up exercise for his flagging creative powers before taking yet another crack at that damn novel. As he worked, fingers practically dancing over the keys, he was hardly aware of the words *"The Ghostwriter"* forming on the page before him. Confidence renewed, he began his story.

Twelve

Journeys of the Mind

Illustrated by Tom Adams

The marriage had lasted less than three weeks. They had been the classic honeymoon couple, bursting with love in their world full of promise.

Richard Hearst had taken his young bride on a fishing trip. He had been wary for he knew that Sarah could not swim, but her delight had overridden his caution and they had spent an idyllic afternoon fishing in a secluded bay about a mile from the harbour. She had taken off her life-jacket to sunbathe and he simply hadn't had the heart to make her put it back on.

Surrounded by cliffs and high rocks, they had been unaware of the growing anger of the sea beyond until the dinghy rounded the jagged headland. Then it was too late.

Neither the dinghy nor Richard Hearst were any match for the maelstrom into which they were sucked. Sarah screamed as the storm lashed and tore at their fragile craft. Drenched by the stinging spray, which shot like hailstones from the crests of the heaving waves, Richard could do nothing but cling to the rudder in a futile attempt to steer a course for land. Then a freak wave exploded into the craft with the force of a cannon ball and the boat capsised, catapulting them into the boiling ocean. Although he tried to beat his way towards Sarah, Richard Hearst was forced to watch helplessly as she drifted away from him, bobbing and riding between the peaks and troughs of the swollen waves. He could hear her terrified voice about the pounding of the sea, and the words that would haunt him for the rest of his days:

"Richard, Richard. You *must* help me." Then with diabolical speed she disappeared – and did not resurface.

Three days later he was called down to identify the body, which had been found washed up on a nearby beach. Sarah was hardly marked and as achingly beautiful as when she had been alive.

The practical details kept Richard going: parents and friends informed, death certificates and coroners' reports signed, the body returned home, the funeral carried out. Richard went through the agony in a hollow trance, inured to the grief of Sarah's family and friends. He could sense the waves of hate from her parents, as if they knew his guilt, but felt nothing for them, for he alone had seen her die.

Richard remembered Sarah's body being lowered into the surprisingly deep grave and obscene thoughts of worms, decay and claustrophobia almost overwhelmed him. Then he remembered the vicar's droning ecclessiastical voice.

"God loves each and every one of us," he had said, "and calls us to His purpose and His time. Neither the young nor the old shall escape the whisper of His summons."

As Richard Hearst left the graveyard with his mother, he was filled with a sudden disgust for life and its perverse creator, for when Sarah had died, he had died. At twenty-five he suddenly had nothing to live for.

His first thought was of suicide. Killing himself would be easy, too easy: a quick slice with a razor, a bottle of pills – god knew his mother had enough – climbing onto the roof and simply stepping into space. But living on without Sarah, living on with the agonising burden of his guilt, the echo of her last desperate cry for help... That would be a fitting punishment – a living death.

The bank for whom Richard worked took a compassionate view of his tragedy and gave him a three-month leave of absence with full pay, but he never returned.

For the first year he lived in a blank haze of tranquilisers and drink but try as he might Richard found himself totally incapable of pushing the memory of Sarah from his mind. Life no longer interested him; he preferred to spend his time wandering aimlessly from bar to bar. Chain smoking, oblivious to the existence of others, he would down glass after glass of whisky until, barely able to stand, he would stagger back to his mother's house in the Fulham area of London and collapse.

Day after day Richard's mother was forced to watch the pitiful degeneration of the son of whom she had been so proud. A kind, plump, comfortable woman, she was no stranger to suffering. Having lost her husband when Richard was five, Mrs Hearst fully understood the desperate pain of bereavement.

The crisis in Richard's life had brought Mrs Hearst to the point of both nervous and financial exhaustion, for Richard soon began borrowing from her to such an extent that she was forced to mortgage her house. Then Richard had a mental breakdown, catalysed by tranquilisers and alcohol, and was referred to the acute admissions ward of Millfield Psychiatric Hospital.

The prognosis was good, Richard's beakdown being attributable to a single traumatic incident, and his psychiatrist felt confident that he could push him gently back into the real word.

Richard spent the first week there drying out from his alcoholism, heavily dosed with drugs to alleviate the symptoms of withdrawal. The need for drink gradually diminished, but his depression proved a much greater problem and he did not respond to the stimulants his doctors prescribed. Also he deliberately kept himself apart from the other patients except at mealtimes and compulsory group therapy sessions. Then he would simply gaze at the carpet and say nothing.

On visiting days his mother would come into the brightly lit ward with the small stream of people from the world beyond, and sit through the uncomfortable hours, consumed with aching compassion for her only child who sat speechless, hardly aware of her presence.

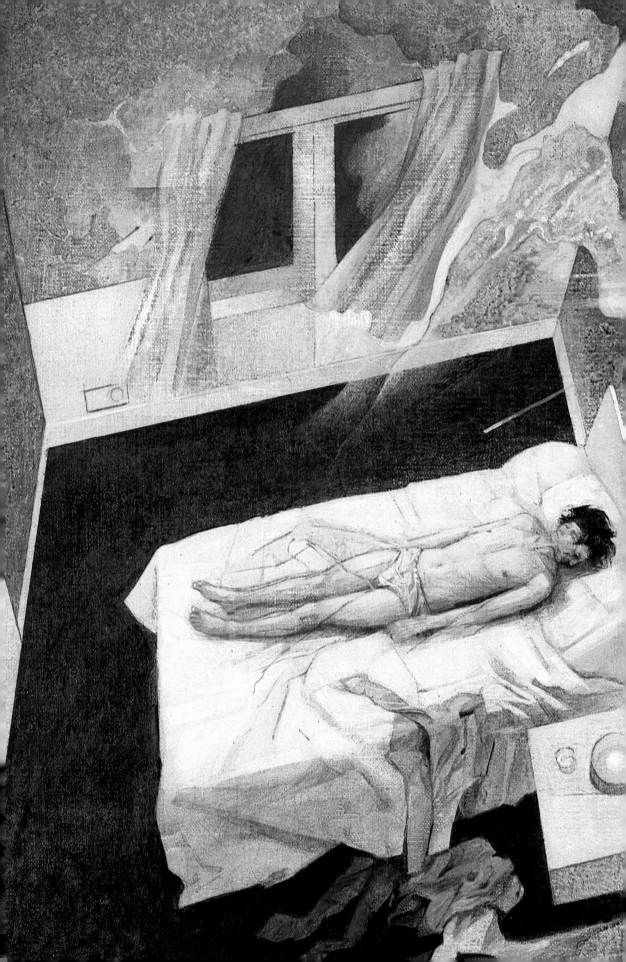

After one such visit she was approached by a nurse and guided into the office where Richard's psychiatrist shook her hand.

"Do sit down Mrs Hearst", he said softly. "I want to talk to you about Richard."

He told her that he was convinced that if the symptoms of Richard's depression could be alleviated psychotherapy would work on the cause. It was therefore his opinion that a course of Electrical Convulsion Therapy should be administered and he asked Mrs Hearst to sign a form giving her consent to the treatment being carried out.

"Does it involve an operation?" she asked nervously.

The psychiatrist explained that E.C.T. was a widespread and radical method of dealing with depression by subjecting the patient to a series of electric shocks. Mrs Hearst looked appalled.

"Don't worry," the psychiatrist said consolingly. Richard will be unconscious – he won't feel a thing."

"And you're *sure* it will help him?"

"I have to be honest and tell you that we don't know or understand how or why the treatment works, but it really is beneficial in a lot of cases. I believe Richard to be one."

The treatment was administered twice-weekly for a month. But it was during the final session that something happened to arouse the first ripple of reaction in Richard since Sarah's death.

As usual his name was called and his stomach knotted as a nurse escorted him into the room. A doctor stood at the head of the treatment couch with a nurse on either side. Behind him was a small brown control box from which wires led to the headset. Richard removed his dressing gown and was helped onto the couch. An anaesthetist approached carrying a syringe.

The intravenous injection flooded into the bloodstream and within a few seconds he was unconscious. The doctor applied the electrodes and, once the nurses had his arms pinned to the couch, switched on the current. Richard's muscles covulsed violently and despite the pressure on his arms he tensed his body, drawing up his knees to a near-foetal position. Then he went limp and was carried to a nearby bed to recover.

But today the effects of the anaesthetic were short-lived and Richard was soon conscious again. Walking back to the ward, still groggy from the whole experience, he desperately tried to recall what it was that happened in the treatment room that now struck him as strange and uncanny. It had all seemed familiar enough – the doctor, nurses, couch, injection, blackout. But what else had happened? Why did some elusive event keep nagging at him to be aknowledged? Then it hit him. Suddenly Richard Hearst realised that he had not only undergone electrical convulsion therapy, – he had also witnessed it! He distinctly remembered seeing himself lying on the couch, seeing himself convulse – of being totally apart from himself. It was an incredible, alarming sensation. Two weeks later Richard Hearst was discharged from the hospital, so impressed were the staff by his new-found optimism. But although his dependence on drugs and alcohol had ceased he remained physically frail and emotionally flat. He had about him a quiet, passive vulnerability common to many who have experienced severe mental collapse.

Richard found it in a Sunday magazine supplement. The article discussed out-of-the-body experiences and the journalist, whilst being traditionally sceptical, handled his subject with sensitivity. He dealt with case histories of people who had experienced leaving their bodies during a temporary death. Then he described those who systematically freed themselves of the physical body by self discipline. On the darker side his research had prompted a warning:

> Those who have successfully escaped their bodies once will often find that they lack the ability to control when it will happen again. Indeed, they often become the victims of a private and repetetive journey into a mixture of hell, ecstasy or sadness.

The warning did nothing to stifle Richard's sense of release. Was it really possible to escape his wretched body and his grey world so full of pain and emptiness? His mind flashed to that moment during his final shock treatment. Yes, it could be done. If only he could escape at will! The article went on to mention that during a journey through the astral plain spirits of loved ones might be encountered if the reciprocal pull was strong enough. What if he should meet Sarah?

Richard felt fired by new energy and as the days passed became more and more obsessed with the notion of freedom. Locked in his room for hour upon hour he willed himself to concentrate on eliminating all thought except that of escape. Then Richard had his first breakthrough. It happened as he lay on his bed one night in a state of deep relaxation. Suddenly a thrumming sound filled his mind and for a few seconds he felt his body dissolve as he plunged helplessly into what seemed a black abyss. Slowly Richard felt himself slip into another dimension, and he was seeing without the use of his eyes.

Richard was floating now – floating above what appeared to be a body lying perfectly still on a bed. Why did it seem so far away? He wanted a closer look and no sooner had the thought occurred to him than he seemed to zoom towards it. Now he was staring directly into the face of the reclinging figure – his own. The realisation that he was looking down on himself made him panic and immediately his new found freedom evaporated and he was once more his body's prisoner.

Thrilled and elated by the experience, Richard knew that if he could successfully control his fear of this new dimension there were no physical limitations on where he could go or what he could see.

Day after day he forced himself to travel further and soon found that he could leave his room and move freely in the darkened streets, entering and leaving places at will. He only had to think of a place and within seconds he was there, looking, experiencing. The desire to return to his heavy body after this release became less and less attractive.

One night, almost fearfully, Richard locked his door, lay down and composed his mind for his journey. He had felt Sarah calling him so strongly throughout the day that he had almost given in to the desire to lie down and escape. However, he sensed that this journey would be a long one and he was afraid that his mother might disturb him. So it was after midnight before Richard felt safe enough to close his eyes and begin the series of disciplines which would ensure the escape from his body.

Sarah alone was real to him, more real than the bed on which he lay, closer than his folded hands, stronger than his own pulse-beat. Suddenly he felt the familiar dropping sensation and was penetrating time and the suburbs, then the sleeping fields, spiralling in a vortex about him.

Richard was helpless – it hadn't been like this before – and suddenly wanted to turn back, to escape from this nightmare, to re-enter his sleeping body and wake. He tried to as he plunged and tumbled deeper into the time warp. Images of earth diffused around him, a large town garish with sodium lights, a huddled village, a broad gleaming reservoir backed by fir woods. Then another village, a spire, a church, a small well-kept churchyard. He passed through grass, sand, gravel and compacted earth. Then he found himself sliding through soft, crumbling wood.

Eventually Richard Hearst found himself at rest. He peered out of ragged eyesockets, along the length of a putrefying corpse. He was not alone; steady soft movement was all around him. The creatures and agents that thrive on the dead were at work – on his beloved Sarah.

Far away the empty shell on the bed arched upwards, then lay still. Few shocks could be so traumatic, few coronaries so massive, so swift.

The abrupt certainty of some disaster wrenched Mrs Hearst awake. She ran up to Richard's room, knocked and called out. Then she summoned her next-door neighbours and a doctor who lived opposite to help her break down the door.

After the hammering and the splintering, the sudden stillness of the room seemed to demand hushed tones. Richard seemed asleep. His hands were folded calmly on his chest, and his closed face wore a patient, waiting look.

"He – he could be sleeping" His mother's voice was hesitant.

The doctor leaned over and felt for the pulse in Richard's neck.

"I'm afraid he's dead," he murmured.

"He's only just died, hasn't he?" sobbed Mrs Hearst. "Something woke me, you see. I know it was Richard. It felt so – so violent. But now he seems quite peaceful, doesn't he? Just a little lost."

Richard opened his eyes to nothing. He was spinning through a silent sensationless void. How long he had hung there in this negative universe he could not tell, days or hours, seconds or centuries. Then he could see blue sky, grass, earth, wood – his own body.

His mother stood white-faced beside it as it lay, its coffin a shiny chrysalis, at the bottom of the open grave, the grave next to Sarah's.

Earth pattered down onto the lid and, as if released from a dark enchantment, twenty-seven years in a prison he could not see, he felt himself soar upwards, upwards through the piercing blue sky and the emptiness of space...

Richard Hearst had embarked on his final journey.